RISE WITH FAITH

Andrea Williamson

To my Father in Heaven, who loves me regardless, strengthens me constantly, and has held me through the most difficult of days. To the One who enabled me to write this book—I pray this comforts those in pain, gives hope to those who need it most, and above all that Your great name is glorified through every word. I will spend the rest of my days loving You and thanking You for Your blessings.

To my three children, who are my entire reason. I couldn't be who I am without you, and I thank each of you for helping heal me with your smiles, laughter and courage, even on your most difficult days. What a gift it is to be your mother. My love for each of you overflows.

To Christopher Lane Williamson, a man who forever changed me and impacted all who knew him. A man who loved hard, sacrificed over and over for his family, worked tirelessly in the job he loved, and who left a legacy incomparable this side of Heaven. His presence brought a light to all who had the pleasure of knowing him, and his passing an emptiness that can never be filled. I will remember you with love, joy and admiration. I dedicate every decision I make for our kids to your memory, and I dedicate this book to the life God blessed us with in each other and our children.

To my family and friends, who love, encourage and help me without hesitation, I will spend the rest of my life loving you and cherishing you all. Your support has been overwhelming, and to know each of you is a blessing in my life. I am so thankful.

CONTENTS

RISE WITH FAITH

Every day is a struggle. Every day. I wake up nervous, longing for the morning to be like it was. I want the nightmare to have ended. It hasn't. I have a reality check with myself and begin to accept it, again. I miss him immensely. I miss the crazy mornings, the texts and calls throughout the day, and wondering what he wants for supper. The afternoons together, juggling practices and ballgames and homework and bedtime. I miss the late-night conversations about the future and dreams and what we want from this crazy life. I miss lying next to his amazing soul every night while we both rest to prepare for the next crazy day, together.

All day, every day, I miss him. I spend every second from morning to bedtime adjusting my mind and believing the truth, and finally coming to an acceptance. Then morning comes and I open my eyes to the same reality. If I could just go back to sleep and wake up in the world in which Chris is still here. Truth floods into me, and another break enters my heart.

But still—I rise that morning, every morning. I rise with courage and hope and face the day, knowing I have faced far worse and made it through and I will make it through this day. I've done this so many days now I know my success rate is one hundred percent on making it through. No matter how many more days I face, I know with God's grace I will endure and decide to find happiness and laughter and purpose in every day. I will pray with my entire being, thanking God for my blessings and every small speck of joy that comes to carry me through.

I will find comfort in knowing Chris is home now, and although I am still here and apart from him, this is a temporary struggle. I will hold onto that truth and hope and promise that I will see him again. I will give everything in me over to Him—my protector, provider, comforter. I will depend on Him to hold me. To carry me. To sustain my weak spirit. I will search for good in everything. Everything. My faith will motivate me, the Lord will guide me, and glimpses of joy will reward me.

I will find peace in knowing that although I can't change my situation, I can always make a choice to strive for the light and to always rise with faith. Always.

"...when I fall, I shall rise; when I sit in darkness, the Lord will be a light to me."

–Micah 7:8

Chapter 1

LIFE BEFORE

Chris was twenty-four and I was twenty when we met in the summer of 1999. I was a junior in college and worked at my dad's business, Johnson's Gym, and he began working out there in late June. He worked full-time as a tree trimmer for the Florence Electricity Department and would come in almost every afternoon around four for a workout. I worked the front desk but was also responsible for cleaning and assisting new members in learning how to use the equipment, and I also taught fitness classes there. Chris and I would speak and sometimes make small talk. He made a great impression on me from the beginning. He was such a polite young man — dark hair, sun-kissed complexion, amazing smile and such a friendly personality. One of those you can't help but like.

I was in a relationship at the time, but Chris and I became friends.

When my relationship ended, and Chris got word of it, he quickly found an opportunity in early December to ask me out. We were standing by the front desk, and Chris was obviously making a point to get a conversation going with me. So he began talking about a band he had recently heard who was going to be back at a local bar soon. He said, "Hey, you should come listen to them sometime. You wanna come with me?" I quickly fired back. "I'm not going to a bar with you!" I wanted to see how badly he wanted this date! "Ok...well why don't you let me take you to get something to eat then?" he offered up as an acceptable alternative. I couldn't refuse. This amazing young man that I had seen for months wanted to spend time with me. My instinct said *say yes*. And so I did.

Our first date was a nervous night for me. I had been in a long-term relationship lasting through high school and into college, and even though I knew Chris somewhat, it had been a long time since I had a first date and the jitters that come with it. He picked me up in his royal blue Ford F-150, and we began our night together, with no idea of how this one decision would help shape our future in such beautiful ways beyond our imagination.

The first stop for the night was Applebee's. I remember what we ate: chicken Caesar salad for me and steak and potatoes for him. What sticks out most in my mind from the restaurant was this: Chris was a huge Alabama football fan, and our date was during a game. There was a television by the bar with the game on, but Chris didn't pay it any mind. He was truly there in that moment with me, cherishing the time to sit one-on-one and just talk to me and us get to know one another. I felt like a priority. And I was impressed. Big time. College football is almost another religion in the South, and when an Alabama fan places spending time with you higher on the priority scale than a game, you take notice. Seriously.

There was a slim selection that night at the movie theater, so we decided to watch *The Bone Collector*, which we joked about later was the least romantic movie we could have seen. We had quite a bit of time between dinner and the movie, so we sat in his truck in the parking lot for a while talking about everything under the sun. It came so naturally for us with each other. I felt like I had known him forever. And he made me feel comfortable. Taken care of. Happy. It was a good night.

I still remember the moment I fell in love with him. Our second date. He was driving us out of town to eat at Olive Garden because he found out that was my favorite place to eat, and at the time the closest one was about ninety miles away. Again, I was feeling high up on the priority scale, and riding for that long gave us a great opportunity to have deep and meaningful conversation. So we were driving along and Chris started talking about life and what he wanted in his. He told me he was at the point in time that he was really ready to grow up and settle down with someone. I just knew at that moment that he wanted that someone to be me. As crazy as it sounds with it being the second time we had even been alone together, I knew he felt the same about me as I did about him. Maybe he told me to see how I would respond. I don't know. We never talked about the conversation later. But even though I didn't say it, looking across the seat at him with his hands on the steering wheel saying those words to me, I realized then that I wanted the same for him. And I wanted it to be with me. I loved his voice, how honest and genuine he was. It was the truth-defining moment for me. *This man, and me, forever.*

After that night we hit the inseparable stage head on. If we weren't around each other at the gym or on a date, we were spending hours on the phone. Oh, young love. When you just want to know every ounce of everything about one another and it's never enough. I so easily became attached to Chris' infectious smile and charming personality. When he walked in the room smiling, he lit it up. Sometimes you can just feel the good in someone. He was good. And genuine. There was a level of maturity there that I appreciated. We fit together well and quickly became best friends.

Chris was such a gentleman. He was honest. He was considerate of my needs. He was strong and was a hard worker. He was funny. And smart. He was a Christian. A country boy. He loved the outdoors. And he looked good too! Most importantly I knew he would someday make an amazing husband and father. He called me beauty queen for a long while. Then it became baby girl. That one made my heart sink. I knew he was the one.

We were so undeniably in love, and by February 4, 2000, we were engaged. Yes, that's right. Two months after our first date we knew we would spend forever together. He asked my dad (and mom) if he could marry me. He drove me to the place we met on that Friday afternoon, and out on the sidewalk of the gym building, he dropped to his knees and asked me. Simple and romantic. Nothing fancy because that wasn't us. But it was perfect. We couldn't have been happier and more at peace with what our future held. Plans immediately began for our wedding. We were so excited.

Spring turned into summer, and we remained busy with classes and work. We wanted to marry as quickly as possible the next year, and with me not graduating until May, we decided on January 6 because I would be in a holiday break and it would give us enough time for a honeymoon. We had no idea what we were doing. We just knew what we wanted. And we knew we would figure it out. All of it. So full plans began unfolding with location and bridal party and attire and the wedding dress. *The* wedding dress. Oh, I could have lived in it. Corset style top with a skirt and a train and a long veil and satin heels. It's really all I needed. We could have married in the pasture with Chris' cows, and as long as I had that dress I probably would have been content. Well, not really. It was perfect for me, but I had dreamed of this day for years, and I wanted the church wedding with the organ and the candles and roses and loved ones. So that's what we would have. All of it. I spent the next several months figuring out how to plan the event and get everything lined up. My mom helped me all the way. All was well. Life was great.

And then it wasn't.

Friday, October 13, 2000. Our first family tragedy. My brother Travis was in a severe car accident as he was struck by an influenced driver who crossed into his lane and hit his vehicle head on. He was twenty-seven.

Chris and I were told by a dear friend of mine about the accident, and we arrived at the crash scene (about three miles from our home) before he was taken to the hospital. We pulled up and Chris said, "Andrea, we need to run because it looks like they already have him in the ambulance." So we did. I remember standing at the back of the opened doors and looking at him. He wasn't moving. I was in shock. Travis had been in car wrecks before. He was always ok. So I guess I thought he was this time. Or at least I hoped. The paramedic told me they had to get him to the ER, and Chris and I quickly got in his truck and followed behind. I saw the paramedics in the back performing CPR on the man I had always looked up to, the man I adored growing up with, riding waves at the beach with, playing in the snow with, opening Christmas gifts with. My big brother. He always looked after me. And protected me. And made me laugh. He told Chris one night in our living room that I was a keeper because I looked good but was low maintenance. He was always coming up with clever things to say, and his laugh was contagious. All of these thoughts flooded my mind as I saw through ambulance windows and tear-filled eyes my brother in need. I'll never get that image out of my mind.

Chris and I arrived at the hospital before anyone else. His mom was bringing my mom, and my dad was out of town a few hours away and hadn't made it back yet. They took me and Chris upstairs to a waiting area, and I remember thinking *please don't let a doctor come here to me right now. Please let my parents get here.* I knew I couldn't tell them what I was fearing. Our moms arrived, and soon after the ER physician came in. He began explaining Travis' internal injuries and that they were just too severe and he hadn't made it through. I remember that experience so vividly. Me, my precious mom, and Chris and his mom, sitting in those waiting room chairs. Shocked. Confused. Distraught. Scared. Chris' mom

Kay said, "I think we should pray," and she led us in the sweetest prayer, asking Jesus to help us and give us strength. The hospital gradually filled with family and friends as the news spread, my sweet daddy and oldest brother Brian arrived, and we all comforted each other the best we could.

After a few hours we left the hospital, without my brother. I climbed into Chris' truck with him and went to the middle of the seat to sit right next to him like I always did. He said, "Andrea, I think you need to sit next to the door so you'll be safer." It's amazing how quickly your mind can shift to fear after tragedy hits.

The next few days were beyond exhausting and painful. My parents faced the unthinkable: burying their child. I was so thankful to have Chris to comfort and encourage me and just be strong for me. I couldn't possibly rely on my parents at the time for that. I felt a responsibility to do it for them. But I needed it too. The night of the accident my dad actually told Chris, "Sleep in there with Andrea. I know I don't have anything to worry about. She needs you. Stay with her." My dad knew I needed that security. And comfort. And he knew he could trust Chris. He was right.

This was a first for our family. We had never lost someone so suddenly and in such a tragic way. I had not even experienced the loss of a close family member until I was sixteen, when my grandpa passed from a lung disease. This was such a difficult time for our family, and my parents especially were grief-stricken. I woke many mornings to the sound of my dad crying. I had never seen him hurt so deeply. And my mom. She and my brother had such a close relationship. She felt lost without him.

I remember hurting so much for my parents, yet not grasping at all what they were going through. I also remember feeling guilty that I would be leaving them soon. I still lived at home the baby of three kids, so I was the only child left there with them. It was such a crazy, overwhelming time. There was so much sadness over losing Travis mixed with so much excitement for my new life.

Plans continued for our wedding the next few months, and we faced the first Christmas without my brother. We began a tradition that Christmas Eve in 2000. We met at the cemetery and sang a few Christmas carols and lit a lantern for Travis. I learned from my parents then to honor and remember our loved ones, and in doing so, to begin to heal.

January 6, 2001. A beautiful Saturday in North Alabama. At a two o'clock wedding at North Wood United Methodist Church, we became Mr. and Mrs. Chris Williamson. We were so happy. And I was so proud of my parents. They held it together so well. I know it had to be overwhelming emotionally, but they put on smiles and gave me an amazing day. There were no doubts in my mind. I was proud to marry Christopher Lane Williamson. I had no idea what our future would hold, but I knew together God would lead us on the right path.

When I walked down that aisle to Chris, nothing else mattered. The tears in our eyes assured us both that we were in this together, always and forever. To have and to hold, for better, for worse, for richer, for poorer, in sickness and in health, to love and to cherish, till death do us part. Forsaking all others, as long as we both should live. Vows that held. Never broken.

After a honeymoon to Jackson Hole, Wyoming, where we skied for the first time and visited Yellowstone on snowmobiles, we settled into our new life together back home. I was in my last semester of my senior year at the University of North Alabama, and Chris was back to his full-time job every day seven a.m. to three-thirty p.m. His tree trimming crew was on call a week every five weeks, so we got accustomed quickly to the middle-of-the-night phone calls and storms leading to fallen trees and overtime hours. Chris' career goal was to become a lineman, and he was going through the right steps up the ladder to get an apprenticeship.

Those first few months of marriage were definitely an adjustment. I had never lived on my own, and neither had Chris until about two months before we got married. We were both hit with challenges and responsibilities we had never experienced. Being a full-time student meant that I could work only part-time at the gym, which wasn't a lot of pay. Money was tight, but we managed. Learning to live together was mostly a smooth transition. I say *mostly* because of course we had issues to work through and compromises to make. But considering the fact that we were adjusting to sharing a home, managing money, paying bills and everything that comes with being newlyweds, we were a great team. We always found a way to laugh, no matter the obstacle. At the end of the day, no matter what, we were lovers and best friends. The best kind of relationship. We were relying on God, and He was blessing us.

I graduated in May with a Communications Degree in

Public Relations, and after a graduation trip to the beach, I immediately began working full-time as the Marketing Director of the Tennessee Valley Art Association (TVAA) the first of June. In July, after waking a few mornings in a hot flash and feeling *different*, I decided to take a pregnancy test. Chris stood there in the bathroom with me watching the results come in. Positive. I'll never forget the smile across his face. I was terrified. He was ecstatic. Chris was so ready to be a dad. We quickly began telling family and friends. After several months and the reality of my tummy growing and movements being felt, reality was becoming crystal clear. Chris and I were going to have new roles in life: mom and dad. It was scary, but we were eager as well. I continued working until a few weeks before my due date. We decided that once she was born, I would work only part-time so I could spend as much time taking care of her as possible. Financially it would be a strain, but we felt it was important, and so I resigned from my position at the TVAA by the end of March. I would go back to working for my dad as office manager of the gym.

We welcomed our baby girl, Averee Faith, on April 19, 2002 at 1:11 a.m. Chris' call out number for work was E-111 (E for electricity and each employee was assigned an identification number with it), so he always thought it was the coolest thing that she was born at that time.

We took our new baby home a few days later, and once again faced responsibilities we had never known. We had no idea what we were doing! We tried our best, though, from the beginning to be the best parents we knew how. Averee sometimes (many times) cried a lot. So sometimes (many times) I cried a lot. There were days Chris would walk in from work with me holding her out for him to hold. I found out quickly how exhausting motherhood was. And looking back I realize how young I was! A twenty-three-year-old mom who had only been a wife for a little over a year. Lots of adjustments happening rapidly. But we were figuring it out, and Chris was naturally great at being a dad. He loved everything about it. She looked like him, which I jokingly acted like bothered me, but I loved that he had that to brag about. We were over the moon for our little girl. She made us a family.

By the fall of that year we began building a house next to Chris' grandparents, and Chris was promoted to a groundman position at the electricity department. He was one step away from his goal. We spent the next several months working on our house. We did as much of the work as possible to save money, with lots of help from family and friends. We moved in by the end of May 2003, a month after Averee's first birthday. We settled in nicely and began enjoying our new home with our baby girl.

In 2004 Chris was thrilled and relieved to be hired as an apprentice lineman. He began classes at the IBEW (International Brotherhood of Electrical Workers) Local Union 558's NJATC (National Joint Apprenticeship Program), where he would attend class for four years. We were so proud for him to start this new career path. It had been his dream. And now it was becoming a reality. He would be a lineman.

In November of that year, after months of prayers and anticipation, we learned we were expecting our second child. Five months later we were excited to find out we would welcome a baby boy this time. Our son, Brody Lane, was born August 11, 2005. Chris was proud to have a son to share his love of hunting and outdoors with. We were now blessed with two healthy children, a girl and a boy. Life was good. Chris' career was in place, and our family was growing in a beautiful way.

No one really warned us what going from one child to two would be like. We definitely experienced a wake-up call. But like other times in our life, we rolled with the punches and kept on going with (mostly) smiles on our faces. There were some stressful times. Small children are stressful. But there was so much joy in our lives to drown out the bad. We always acted crazy with the kids and made sure there were lots of laughs in our house. By the time Brody was one, we were pros at having small kids. Or so we thought.

Things got easier as Averee was preschool age and Brody was a toddler. They were such good kids. Averee was becoming a little ball player, which pleased her daddy. He became very involved with helping her in the yard and helping coach her softball and soccer teams. And Brody was into the outdoors and tractors and guitars and country music. Everything his daddy loved. We were such proud parents.

In the spring of 2007, we got an amazing surprise of finding out we were expecting our third child. We felt overwhelmed but trusted God's plan for our family. Thank the Lord we survived because it truly does take a village, and between help from our parents and Chris' grandparents and my grandmother, our kids hit the jackpot (as did we).

In August of that year, Averee began kindergarten. We decided after much prayer and discussion to send her to a private Christian school. We knew it would be a constant sacrifice, but we wanted it for our children and decided we would do whatever necessary to financially make it possible.

Fall rolled into the holidays, we welcomed a new year, and on January 3, 2008, three days before our seventh wedding anniversary, our baby girl Lilly Grace completed our family. We were officially outnumbered.

It was a memorable childbirth experience. Chris had begged my obstetrician with all three pregnancies to let him catch the baby during delivery. My doctor had told him after Brody was born that if we had a third he might. He told Chris it was a little different than delivering a calf. I agreed. So we were at the moment where the nurse said to me, "Keep your legs down and let me go get the doctor. Do not push." Chris started in on me. "Andrea, when he comes in be sure and tell him you don't mind me delivering her. Ok?" I said, "I don't care right now who delivers her as long as you get her out!" So my doctor came in and Chris started working on him. He gave in and told Chris to get cleaned up and put some gloves on. He let Chris sit on the stool and everything and gave him instructions on shoulders and honestly I don't know what else because my only job was to push and hope someone was there and ready. And he was. So this amazing miracle from God made her way into the world with her daddy as the first to touch, hold and welcome her. It was perfect. He was a pro. I guess the calf deliveries helped after all.

She was born on a Thursday night, which was Chris' school night at the union hall. He was only a few months from completing the apprenticeship program and had been sure to be in class every time, so he could get perfect attendance. It was all about a gold watch that has been in my jewelry box ever since. But it was important to him to get it. Lilly was born at 6:05 p.m. and his class had started at 5:30. After all the after birth things had taken place — the cleaning of the baby, visits from her new brother and sister and all of the rest of our family, the first feeding and everything settling down — Chris looked at me. "Well, do you think it would be ok for me to run over to school to at least make an appearance? I'll be late but they will still count me as attending." I told him to go on, that we were good. That's such a funny memory to me, but it shows his priorities: family first and then being a hard worker and taking pride in his career. Of course I always brought it up when I could through the years: "I had just birthed our child and you ran off to get a watch!" We loved to pick at one another.

In May of the same year, Chris completed his apprenticeship program and became a topped-out lineman. We were so proud. He loved his job. He was good at it and was highly respected. He loved being outdoors and helping others, and this allowed him to do both. As someone who was responsible for regular day-to-day work hours, along with restoring power after storms and wintry weather, he worked many long hours and sometimes missed holiday gatherings and special events.

When Lilly was almost two, he got called to work on

Christmas Eve night. He didn't have to go as he wasn't on call, but he knew they needed his help, so he went. That was my first experience at being Santa alone. He made it back at four o'clock Christmas morning, had just enough time to take a shower and lay down, and Averee was awake by five. He didn't even tell her to go back to bed. He just got up and went in the living room and acted excited with her. We went through the entire day of three family get-togethers, and he finally got to sleep that night once we had made it back home and of course after he had spent some time with the kids looking through their Christmas goodies.

Chris was such an amazing dad with his priorities in the right place. He always spent a great deal of time one-on-one with the kids. He was always the one working with Averee on softball, practicing baseball and football with Brody, and singing and cutting up with Lilly. So many days he would come home after a long day of work, and although he was exhausted, he would immediately go out with one of the kids to throw ball. Chris wanted to be present in their lives and never wanted them to doubt his love for them. He told me a few times that he wanted his kids to look back in their adulthood and remember him as the daddy that took time with them no matter what. After long days of working in the Alabama scorching heat, he could have easily come in and sat in the air conditioning and relaxed. But he always placed their needs first. They needed time with their daddy, and so they had it.

The next several years were spent at ballgames and preschool functions, beach and Disney World vacations, and doing improvements to our house. We had gotten used to being a family of five even though we both felt like we were in a circus most of the time. It was a good circus but still a circus. Controlled chaos is an accurate description. Don't get me wrong, I loved it. We loved it. Our life was filled with joy. Busy, crazy, rewarding joy.

We lost a few immediate family members to sicknesses in 2009 and 2010. In April of 2009, Chris' granddaddy "Paw" passed from a lung disease. We lived next door to that set of grandparents and were very close to them. Chris always said Paw was his hero, and his passing changed Chris in many ways. Then in 2010 my aunt Angela, who I was extremely close to, and was more like an older sister to me, passed away suddenly from a blood clot in her aorta. The next month my uncle Terry, who suffered brain damage during childbirth and had lived with us my entire childhood, passed from Parkinson's. So those two years were emotionally challenging as we learned to live life following the loss of three important parts of our lives. We learned to truly appreciate every moment even more and just to be more thankful and content.

In May of 2013 Chris signed a Journeyman Lineman Service Truck position with the Florence Electricity Department. By now we had two kids in private school, and Lilly would begin the coming fall. My mom and I had our own business, Impulse, a women's boutique in a local shopping mall, but even with my pay and Chris' salary and overtime hours, money was tight at times. He had always anticipated that promotion, and when one of his friends retired and the position became available, Chris jumped at the opportunity. He was excited to have another week on call in addition to his on-call hours with his line crew. The extra overtime hours meant a great deal more income for our family. That was his motivation. He didn't enjoy being on call and going out all hours of the night to work, but he knew it would help his family. So he did it.

His duties included installing new overhead electrical services, investigating trouble calls, correcting problems, and much more. A week every four weeks he would have a company service truck to drive all week and be on call from Friday to Friday. He worked lots of hours during that week, and there was no definite schedule for him. It was difficult for us when all three kids had activities and he couldn't help take them or pick them up, or sometimes even be there. He had to be with the service truck twenty-four hours a day during his call week and had to stay close to home in case of a call-out.

We managed with help from our parents and grandparents and friends. Chris felt so guilty not being as present during those weeks. I always told him I was perfectly fine with him giving up the position at any time. We had talked a few times during the year about him coming off the service truck by the fall of 2014. Averee would begin junior high and be playing school ball, and Chris was concerned with missing ballgames and school functions. He knew our kids would be young only once, playing ball once, going through school once, growing up once. He loved his job, but he loved us more. He didn't want our kids to grow up thinking work and money was more important than them. He was just trying to be the best provider and a hard-working husband and father, and he was.

That year, 2013, was a great one for us. After twelve years of marriage and the stresses of change and money and losing loved ones and raising small children, we were at such an amazing, peaceful place in our relationship. We had always been great friends, but of course we had difficult times, times that we weren't always happy and were just too stressed with life. After a few challenging years, we gained such an amazing appreciation for each other and our family and where we were. There was such comfort between us, and our love had matured in such a great way. We were best friends and rarely had a disagreement. It was so rare, in fact, if we ever did disagree on something Brody would say, "You and dad aren't getting a divorce are you?" I always thought that was so funny because we didn't even raise our voices to each other. But the kids weren't used to being around arguing, so he automatically thought we must be about to separate if we were. Even in times of not seeing eye-to-eye, we respected one another with deep admiration. At this point in our lives and marriage, we appreciated our differences and realized how much we truly depended on one another. Financially we were finally in a comfortable place and didn't stress every month about bills. We were relieved and blessed.

In the fall of 2013 we had our second annual Wild Game Dinner at our church, Cross Point Church of Christ, and it had increased substantially in funds raised from the previous year. Cross Point hosts a toy and coat giveaway every December to provide new toys, coats, Bibles and prayers to hundreds of needy families in our community. For a few years Chris had spent hours during the night talking to and praying with families that were waiting to get into the giveaway. The giveaway doors always opened on the first Saturday in December, and families would start lining up on the sidewalk outside beginning Friday. He and a group of guys at church would go up on Friday night, put up plastic on each side of the sidewalk hanging down from the awning, put out heaters, and just spend time there all night with them. Chris was blessed by it. It touched his heart to hear their stories, and he felt led to do more.

In July of 2012 Chris had met with one of the ministers about the idea for a wild game event to raise funds for the giveaway. The giveaway had been funded every year by donations from church members and those in the community. As a hunter and outdoorsman, Chris had attended similar events over the years and thought it would go over well in our area. Once approved, he talked with friends at church and in the community to get them involved, and planning began. With only eight weeks to get everything together — speaker, food, giveaway items, silent auction items, sponsors and ticket sales — we were thrilled to have raised $8000. Chris was so proud. I remember sitting in our bed and him standing in the doorway, talking about how he had finally *found his place* at church in such a great way doing something he loved helping others. His life felt meaningful in a new way.

Our second event in 2013 was more successful and raised around $11,000. Plans began for a third event for 2014, and Chris talked to and booked a speaker. He also drew out a design for the t-shirts. He had no idea that would be the last event he would be

27

involved in planning. He also would have never envisioned that this event, renamed the Chris Williamson Wild Game Fest, would raise $25,000 in 2014 and $27,000 in 2015 and 2016.

In October of 2013 on the weekend of Halloween, we took a trip to Gatlinburg, Tennessee to visit the Smoky Mountains with Chris' dad Gary, stepmom Tammra, and his sister Heather and her family. What a memorable trip! We stayed in a cabin on a mountain, had several visits from a grizzly bear family, spent a day at Cade's Cove, and then there was a day at Dollywood. Chris was like a little kid with those roller coasters. I had never seen him so giddy about rides before. I've never been a big fan of them, especially the ones that go upside down. He was just so excited that I couldn't say no. And if he rode one before me he would say, "Come on, Andrea! It's not bad at all." And of course to me it was horrible. Every time he talked me into coming on one with him, as soon as the roller coaster started I would think *I'm seriously not gonna make it off this. This is the end for me.* And he thought it was hilarious. We had such an amazing trip that weekend. We had always loved the mountains.

The holidays brought on just as much joy as always. Thanksgiving was spent running our family around to several family get-togethers stuffing food in our faces, watching parades and dog shows on television, and throwing football and catching up with everyone. Then Christmas rolled around with multiple gatherings and lots of gifts and food. We were thankful Chris wasn't on call but talked about how the next year he would have the service truck on Thanksgiving and Christmas, which we dreaded.

We had a great Christmas day, with excited kids and the typical day of running from one house to another, visiting with as much family as possible, and loading our car with goodies we received at each home. As always, we made it back home that evening and began unloading all our gifts and eating lunch leftovers my mom would always bring by for us to have. We were always so exhausted Christmas night, and of course the kids were still going strong, motivated by wanting to enjoy all the new toys and gadgets they had received. Chris and Brody kept their tradition alive that night of working whatever Lego project Santa had brought. They looked forward to that every year.

A few weeks later came the New Year and celebrating Lilly's sixth birthday, and our thirteen-year wedding anniversary. The year 2014 was looking to be a wonderful one for the Williamson family. The kids were doing well and beginning their second half of the school year, Averee in the sixth grade, Brody in second, and Lilly in kindergarten. We were anticipating the spring and in deep discussion of putting in a pool for the summer.

After the first few months of the year when we actually experience really cold temperatures in Alabama, spring was upon us. The kids had spring break the last week of March, and Brody had recently developed somewhat of an obsession with Elvis Presley. He had been begging us to take him to Graceland, so we picked a day that week to go and Chris took the day off work. Chris wasn't much of an Elvis fan, but he was excited to let Brody have that experience. So we loaded up the family, and my mom and dad and niece also joined us there. It was a fun day. I think Chris became an Elvis fan that day. He was certainly enjoying looking at all the exhibits and letting Brody take a few dozen pictures on his phone. We enjoyed burgers and fries at the fifties-style diner there and then headed home. We didn't need fancy vacations together. Just time.

April brought baseball and softball practices and games in full force for Brody and Averee, Averee had her twelfth birthday, and I turned thirty-five. April is always our biggest storm and tornado month in Alabama, and it didn't disappoint that year. The Madison/Huntsville area, which isn't far from home, experienced a great deal of damage from a tornado on April 28, and Chris was on the service truck that afternoon working about 50 miles west of it, as other areas were experiencing damage as the storm came through. I remember talking to him on the phone, and for the first time being really concerned about where he was in relation to a storm. He had certainly worked out in them before, but being that close to a very strong tornado was concerning me more than usual. I prayed and he worked, got plenty of overtime hours, and came home safe and sound.

May 2014 was a busy month. Brody was busy with baseball, Averee was playing travel softball, and the kids were anticipating school dismissing for summer vacation and our upcoming beach vacation. We were also anxious for Lilly's cast to come off her arm. She had broken it in April at a ballpark where Averee was playing in a softball tournament. It was a bad night. We had been at ballgames all day that Saturday, and as the last ballgame started that night Lilly fell in the grass running back to us from the playground. She came over to us crying hysterically, and after I slid her jacket off and looked at her left arm I said, "Chris, it's broken." Her forearm looked like a C. We rushed her to the emergency room, and Chris held her in his lap in the waiting room. Once it was confirmed that there was indeed a broken bone, Chris went in to watch the orthopedic doctor, one of our friends from church, reset the bone while she was sedated. Things like that didn't bother him. I would have gotten sick. He loved his girl and wanted to see that she was well taken care of.

Her cast finally came off May 19th, we celebrated Chris' thirty-ninth birthday on the twenty-first, school dismissed for summer on the twenty-second, and Brody's baseball season ended, all in the same week. We couldn't have been more excited for summer and our annual family beach trip with my mom, dad, brother and his family, and my cousin. We also had plans for the pool to begin the end of June and we were ready. We always talked about wanting a pool, and it became a joke for us to say, "Maybe next year!" But now it was happening THIS year. Everything was as it should be. Excitement was in the air. We were comfortable with our lives and had everything lined up the way we had planned. Life was good.

On June 2nd we left Orange Beach coming back home after our family vacation. What a great trip we had! Twelve of us in the same condo for four days, enjoying homemade breakfast every day, lots of sand and sun, crab-hunting, seafood restaurants, shopping and just getting lots of relaxation with the Johnson family.

There were a few differences in this year's trip and the

previous ones. Every time we ate on this trip, no matter how loud or busy the restaurant or how hungry we were after wave jumping and beach football throwing, Chris asked Brody to say a prayer before we ate. It's not that we didn't pray before meals, but it was even in the busiest of places, which was unusual.

Also, on trips Chris was always wanting to hurry up and get to the destination, or in a hurry to get back home. Not on this trip. We met for breakfast that morning with the rest of the family before driving towards home and took our time. We stopped for lunch at Peach Park and again, took our sweet time. No hurry at all this trip. I remember at the time thinking that was unusual.

Driving home, I posted a picture on social media of Chris with the kids with the remark "my loves." I'm so thankful that I made that post, showing Chris my love for him and our children. I had taken the picture the night before while we were waiting to play putt-putt. We were sitting on the bench together, and I thought *I should get up and take their picture.* And so I did. I stood up and took a picture of Chris with his babies. His pride and joy. It's my favorite picture. The sunset behind them. Such a small act at the time but now a priceless treasure. A reminder to ALWAYS take the picture. You'll only regret the ones you didn't take.

This was also the night Brody recorded his first cd, singing an Elvis song in a karaoke booth. Chris guarded the door while he sang, to be sure no one interrupted or distracted him. He and Chris had gone out to the car before we left the arcade that night to listen to it, and Brody was disappointed. He didn't think he did a good job and didn't want anyone else to listen to it. But on the drive home while the kids were napping, I snuck it in the cd player. Of course it woke Brody up and he didn't want me to hear it, but Chris bragged on him. He was proud.

There was lots of discussion on our way home about the pool and making last minute decisions so I could let the builder know exactly what we wanted. It was funny because I would ask Chris what he wanted and he would grin and say, "Whatever makes you happy." It became a joke with us. It was so funny to me because I thought *well this is new!* In getting prepared for the pool some trees in the back yard had to be cut, and Chris and his friend Phillip took care of that before our trip. Gary, Chris' dad, wanted the wood, so Chris called him to see if he wanted to come out once we got home to chop it and load it. I remember thinking *why is he worried about that today?*

We made it home around four that afternoon, and Chris said he was going out to cut the grass. While he was out, his mom arrived next door to visit his grandmother, Maw, and he drove the lawnmower over. I was spraying off the back porch with the water hose and looked over to see him sitting on the mower, kicked back with his hands behind his head, talking to his mom while she sat on the back porch. Kay left, and then later his dad, stepmom Tammra, and brother Billy came. Chris and Billy chopped wood, and they and Gary loaded it into the bed of the truck. I remember so vividly looking out the kitchen window and watching those three men work together. Chris had been struggling with back pain the previous weeks, and I remember thinking that all the chopping was going to be bad for him. After we returned from the beach I never heard another mention about back pain. It was unusual in a great way. A blessing indeed.

They left and Chris then decided to go out to our garden to hoe. He was the gardener of the family. I always told him, "You plant it and I'll cook it." The kids loved doing it every year. I've never seen more excited kids than when they got to dig up potatoes. Or carry baskets of tomatoes and cucumbers and peppers and squash to the house. And Brody Lane got ecstatic over a growing watermelon. It was rewarding for them to see the result of the work. Chris took such pride in it. He was always a hard worker, but when he told me this day that he was going out to work in the garden I thought *is he not tired because I am!* The man had driven us all the way home from the beach, cut the grass, chopped wood, and was now hoeing the garden spot. He just couldn't seem to get enough done that day.

I walked out to the garden, and we talked for a few minutes. It was almost sunset. Chris was at such peace. I felt like the vacation had really revived his spirit. He was so calm and relaxed about everything in a way I had not witnessed before. I firmly believe God was putting everything in place. This was the only day that week that Chris would have been able to do that work at our house and the only day he would have been able to see and visit with his parents. What a blessing!

By Tuesday, June 3rd, it was back to summer reality for us. Chris went back to work, and I took Averee to the doctor for swimmer's ear that had gotten worse and was now causing a fever. We had attempted to treat it ourselves with alcohol and peroxide at the beach condo, but nothing seemed to help. She loved the ocean so much she would literally sit in the water and let the waves cover her head (and ears) for hours at a time. So she always ended up with clogged ears. We got antibiotics and drops for her and were hoping she would feel better that afternoon. She had junior varsity summer softball scrimmage games later, and we were excited to see her representing her school for the first time as she prepared for seventh grade. Thankfully the fever broke, and she felt relief.

The games started at 3:30, the same time Chris got off work. He always did everything possible to not miss one of the kids' programs or games. He managed to get gone from work a little early and made it on time. I wasn't surprised. He gleamed with excitement. All the investment he had made with her — batting cage sessions, hitting lessons, throwing in the front yard, all stars and lots of practice — had helped her prepare her for this moment. Softball was his and Averee's thing. I had never pitched a softball with her. It was special for them, their bonding time.

Being the worrying mom, I was afraid she wouldn't do well because she had felt horrible with that ear all day. Well, she played better than she did with good ears! I can't remember if she had five or six at-bats over the two games, but every time but the one when she was walked she smacked the ball to the outfield. All of them were big hits! She had never had that many big hits in two games before. Talk about a proud daddy, smiling ear to ear. Every time she would walk up to the plate he would say, "Here we go, A!" He was soaking every second in, watching his baby girl play in her school's uniform for the first time.

The games ended, and Chris and the kids headed home. I headed over to my boutique to do some work and then to get groceries. As soon as we all left, he called me. He bragged on her like never before: "Andrea, she made such a good first impression!" I remember hearing such pride in him. "I mean she smacked that ball!" He couldn't say it enough. Averee had always been a good softball player, but we had never seen her hit like that. I'm convinced it was a gift from God to her to know how well she did and the pride on her daddy's face that day because his approval was gold to her. It was another great day for us that week.

The next day was a Wednesday. We had not been to mid-week service at church in a long while. We were just crazy busy, and it seemed that most weeks it was the only calm night we could spend at home as a family. Chris called on his way home from work and asked, "We going to church tonight?" I said, "Well, yeah let's go." He said, "Andrea, we need to get back to going on Wednesday," and I agreed.

We arrived at service at 6:30 and walked in together. We talked to a few friends on the way in and had a few laughs, and Chris talked to a few guys about going frog-gigging to get frog legs for the upcoming wild game event. We found seats and worship began. We always enjoyed our Peak of the Week service with lots of singing and inspirational videos and speakers and prayers.

A few things that really stuck out in my mind from that night: Usually during an hour-long church service, Chris' phone would go off at least once with a notification and he would look at it. He and his best friend Les sold sunglasses on eBay so his phone was always going off either with a message or sale notification. But it never came out of his pocket this night. It was completely ignored. Also, Chris always sang out at church, but I've never experienced him singing like he did that night. From the very depths of his soul. I looked at him and thought to myself *wow, he is really singing tonight. He's singing like I've never heard before. We have to be here every Wednesday from now on.* I wanted to freeze that moment of us, together, worshipping God. It was the closest I had ever seen Chris to God, the Holy Spirit visibly working in him. What a blessing!

The other wonderful thing is that sitting there during service with him, I put my arm through his while we sang. I had never done that before. At one point I pulled my arm out to get something out of my purse. As soon as I sat back up, he nudged me a little with his arm wanting me to put mine back through his. I am in love with that memory. Once service ended and after we spent some time talking to several friends on the sidewalk and in the parking lot, Chris headed home with the kids, and I headed over to my store to do a few things before going home.

I'm so proud that on that June 4th night, we were at service together, not just going through the motions, but worshipping with our emotions, the way it should be. Everything was right in our world physically, emotionally, and most importantly, spiritually. We were complete.

Chapter 2

THE STORM

Thursday, June 5th, 2014.

This is everything I can remember. Our alarm went off on a typical summer morning, and we got up at 6:15 to a sunny day. Chris showered while I packed his lunch for him. I always packed his lunch for him. Sometimes he was tired of salads and sandwiches and bought a lunch. But still, I always packed it in case he needed it. He got dressed and came in the kitchen to put his phone and wallet and pocket knife and loose change in his pants pockets. We talked for a few minutes, and he grabbed his lunchbox, kissed me goodbye, and headed to work around 6:35. He texted me a little after 7 to let me know he would be on the service truck that day instead of with his crew, so he would be working until 4:00 that afternoon instead of 3:30.

The kids and I had a usual out-of-school summer morning—them sleeping late, breakfast, television and just hanging out and playing. I spent the morning cleaning and catching up on inventory orders for my store. Chris and I talked and texted a few times that morning about Averee's softball schedule and just day-to-day things. He called me at lunch, and I remember that conversation pretty well. Mostly, I remember his great mood. I could hear the smile on his face. One of his co-workers and best friends was in New York City on a vacation, and Chris was telling me about the conversation they had earlier: "Andrea, I talked to Phillip, and he was standing in Times Square! Can you imagine him being there?!" He was so tickled about it. We both were and I said, "I bet that's a sight to see!" We had such a good laugh about it.

The kids and I had lunch and then got dressed to head into town. Averee had a basketball workout for school ball, and Brody had a haircut appointment. Lilly didn't want to go, so I asked Maw if she could stay next door with her for a few hours. She was always so willing to help me. So Lilly stayed there, I dropped Averee off at the gym at school, and Brody and I did some shopping and then got his hair cut. It was then time to pick Averee up, and we headed home.

I talked to Chris on the way home, and he was telling me that softball practice that night for Averee had been cancelled. The forecast called for storms. Chris and I were surprised practice had already been cancelled since it was still a few hours away. But I mentioned to him that it was very dark toward our house driving up the highway. There was definitely a storm coming.

The kids and I got home and unloaded what we had picked up from shopping that day. I began cooking supper, which was unusually early for us. The wind was picking up, and the sky was darkening. Thunder and lightning increased. I smelled something strange coming from the air vent in the kitchen, like something burning, so I cut the unit off and called Chris. It was a little after four. There was no answer, but he called back a few minutes later. "Hey, I'm sorry. I was at the bank and left my phone in the truck." He was on his way home. I told him what was going on with the unit, and he said he would call John, a friend and repair man. He also said he would look at it as soon as he got there. At this point we thought we were going to be spending a night at home together as a family.

We never anticipated Chris having to go back to work once he got home. He wasn't on call. Yes, he sometimes had to work when he wasn't, if there was too much storm damage for the on-call crews to handle. It just didn't seem like it would be that bad. It was. We hung up, and about fifteen minutes later the land line phone rang. It was dispatch. I told him he would have to call Chris' cell phone because he hadn't made it home yet. So, I knew when Chris got home he was going to have to leave. If he hadn't have been almost home, he would have turned around and headed straight back. Thank the Lord he was almost home.

He walked in the back door after walking out to look at the air unit. He told me he had to head back in to work, and I said, "Yeah, I know, he called you here first." We had a good laugh when I told him the dispatcher had forgotten who he called and said, "Is uh, uh," and I said, "Chris?" He said "yeah yeah Chris!" It was around four-thirty. He rubbed Brody's head as he walked into the kitchen and said, "I sure do like that haircut, Bro!" He was in the happiest mood. I asked him if he would please sit down and eat a bite before he had to go. He said he would. Normally he would have said he had to go and to save some for later. I asked him what he wanted to drink and was a little disappointed that he wanted tea because there was enough left for one glass and I kind of wanted it. I'm so glad he got it. He always bragged on my sweet tea.

We sat down at the table together, and Chris asked Brody to say a prayer. There was the usual small talk conversation but a little more rushed because Chris had to leave soon. By 4:45 he was getting ready to leave. Our night at home together as a family had been shortened to fifteen minutes. He made a few phone calls before leaving to get himself a helper. He was going to be on the service truck when he went back in, so it would just be him and a truck operator working together.

I hugged and kissed him with the usual, "I love you. Be careful." I was following him through the hall to see him out when Brody called to him from the living room. "Dad, how long you gonna have to work?" Chris enthusiastically said, "I don't know, son, but I hope I work all night!" He wasn't usually excited about working when he wasn't on call. He was that night.

Chris walked out the door into the garage of our home we had built together. He walked out to his new white Ford F-150 that he was so proud to have bought when he got the service truck position, climbed in, closed the door, and pulled out of our driveway.

I feel guilty that I wasn't worried in the least bit when he left us that warm June fifth night. Oh there had been so many times I had done my share of worry, times that he had worked so many hours I didn't understand how the man could stand, let alone work.

I worried when he would work all day, all night, come home and sleep for five or six hours and go back again. I was always in awe of that. The strength and ability to just keep going, even beyond exhaustion.

When he went to Kentucky in 2009 to help restore power after an ice storm, I worried until he made it back that cold February afternoon. That was the first time he had been away from us that long and my first experience as a single mom at home with three kids. I was working and not expecting him until that night, sitting in the office at my store and in walked Chris, wearing that little mischievous grin. He always loved surprises. Especially if he was the one surprising.

I worried plenty when he was in Long Island, New York in 2012, working to restore power after Hurricane Sandy. When he finally made it back home, after the longest week of my life that November, I remember standing in the door watching those headlights and my exhausted husband finally arrive. I had never been so relieved and happy to see him. He was safe. And sound. And home. With us. He told me later that the look in my eyes (along with the tears coming out of them) and the tight squeeze he felt around him reassured him of just how much I loved and appreciated him. I'm so glad he knew.

He called me a few more times letting me know that John was coming out to check the unit and then followed up while John was working on it.

7:26 p.m. — the last time Chris called. We talked for one minute and spoke the words we always ended a conversation with:

"I love you."

The kids and I had been watching *Finding Nemo* since the bad weather had kept us inside. John finished up checking the unit, explained to me what was going on, and that he would be back with the parts in a day or two to repair it. So, we would be extra warm downstairs for a day or so. John left.

At 8:30 p.m. the phone rang. Caller I.D. showed Chris' mom's cell number. My hello was quickly overcome by her distraught voice. I'll never forget it. Complete panic and worry. "Andrea, what has happened to Chris?! Someone called me. He's at the emergency room! I'm driving there now." I said, "What?! Kay, I don't know! I don't know. I'm on my way. I just have to…have to get the kids taken care of." I hung up the phone, and it immediately rang again. My parents' number. "Andrea. It's daddy. Momma and I are coming to get you to take you to the hospital." "Daddy, I don't know what is happening. Kay called. He's hurt. I don't know." My dad told me that a co-worker had called my brother Brian, and he had called my dad. No details, just that he was hurt and at the hospital.

We hung up, and I was left with three anxious kids that had been listening to these conversations about their rock, their daddy. They needed answers, and I couldn't provide them. I began internally praying for strength to not hit my knees in our house and fall apart in front of these babies of ours. I began talking to them as calmly as possible that daddy was hurt and at the hospital, and I was going to have them stay at Maw's house while I went to him. I hated so badly to ask it of her since I knew the worry she was experiencing as well. But at that moment she was my option of not exposing them to what I had no idea they might be exposed to. *I couldn't take them there if...no.* My mind couldn't go there.

I walked the kids next door to Maw's house and hugged and kissed them before my parents pulled up. I hated to leave our kids. My gut was experiencing the worst pain it had ever felt, but I was displaying all the hope I could for them. Lilly was the last to go inside. She said, "Please, God, let Daddy be ok." I remember the excruciating pain in my heart that I couldn't assure her. And the fear that quickly flooded in of *what if I can't come home with their daddy? What if he isn't ok? Please, dear Lord, let him be ok. Please.*

Here were the thoughts that had been swirling in my mind since Kay's phone call: *If Chris were in ANY way capable, he would be on the phone with me telling me he was ok. If his body was so badly injured but he was conscious and able to speak, he would have someone holding the phone to his mouth to say, "I'm ok."* He knew what a worrier I was. There's no way he would let me worry the unthinkable.

Riding in the car with my parents on the way to the hospital, the panic was really starting to set in and take residence in my heart and mind. The hope in me was trying to believe he was just unconscious or that they wouldn't let him call me, that he was going to be alright. I've always been an optimist. But my soul. It was deeply hurting. My head. It was spinning. My entire being was thinking and praying and worrying and stressing and just scared. There was more dread in me than ever before. It was consuming me. Along with fear. Fear of another excruciating tragedy. I begged God for the opposite.

The unimaginable reality that I didn't know yet was that Chris had climbed a pole in the backyard of a house on Arlington Boulevard in Florence, Alabama to restore power to that Hickory Hills neighborhood, and after accidentally coming in contact with an energized 7200-volt line, was immediately taken to Heaven to be with our Lord.

My dad pulled up to the entrance of the Eliza Coffee Memorial Hospital Emergency Room and let me and my mom out while he parked. I remember so well rushing through those doors and immediately looking for someone. Anyone. A familiar face. Someone to tell me that Chris was hurt, or just unconscious, but ok. Or maybe in surgery. Or ICU. Or recovery. I was desperately longing for a voice to say, "Andrea, he's ok." All I wanted and needed was an *everything's ok* moment, a moment where all the fear and dread and panic and worry could just vanish and be replaced with hope and relief. But it couldn't be found.

There were no familiar faces outside or in the waiting room. I knew that was bad. One of Chris' co-workers was waiting for us and said, "We have to go back this way." Bless his heart. What a heavy burden for him although knowing him I know he wouldn't have had it any other way. I didn't even ask him what was going on. I couldn't speak. The words just wouldn't come out of me. All I could do was manage to put one foot in front of the other to walk what seemed like an eternity down the hallway. My mom asked how Chris was, and he said, "We just have to keep going back this way." He couldn't say the words. He couldn't be that messenger. My heart sank more in that moment. I knew.

We finally made it to where family and friends were gathered in a hallway, and I looked at Kay. No one had to tell me he was gone. The complete anguish filling that room combined with everything else was so loud it was literally screaming this unthinkable truth. Oh, how I wanted to deny it and force it to go far far away! And in that moment my world began to spin. When I say that, I literally felt like I was in an uncontrollable spiral that wouldn't stop, trapped in a twister of anguish and fear and shock and brokenness and desperately wanting so badly to escape its emotional destruction. But there was no escape. There was no running away from this. No waking up. No different result. No change of fate.

It's crazy how in such life-altering moments we know the facts but our hearts can't comprehend. *Was this really happening? How was this happening? How can I change it? Why, why, why?* Even with the tragic way I lost my brother and the losses of other close family members that were extremely difficult, I have never been so consumed and overwhelmed by grief as I was this night. It came in waves of uncontrollable sobbing, followed by numbness and shock. Repeat.

I remember familiar faces coming in and embraces and crying and my mind constantly thinking of the kids. Oh, our babies. *How was I going to look in their sweet faces?* They were my biggest concern. I was waiting for them to tell me I could see Chris, or I would have left soon after to get to them. I couldn't let them find out before I got home. I was so afraid of relatives or friends calling Chris' grandmother or going to her house once they heard the news. She still didn't know. Then there was social media to worry about. I asked my mom to leave and get them from Maw's and take them home, to keep anyone from telling them, to protect them. I knew she could handle it emotionally and would do what I needed her to do. Chris' cousins were going to get Maw and bring her to the hospital.

Over the next hour or so, lots of family, church members, and Chris' co-workers and friends had gathered in the hallway to show their love and support. I remember standing up to hug a few of the guys from the electricity department when they came in. I wrapped my arms around each one of them holding their wet, dirty work uniforms, and all I wanted was for one of them to be Chris. Oh, how I wanted that. I longed to see him walk in and say, "What's going on here? I'm perfectly fine! This is all a mistake. Everything is ok." I just needed my husband's arms around me telling me all was right in the world. His comfort was what I needed. His presence. His wet dirty clothes and mud covered boots on his strong, perfectly fine body. That's what I needed. To be able to put him in the car with me, take him home to our babies, and live happily ever after. I needed my Chris.

After waiting for what seemed like forever, we were asked for immediate family to move into a private waiting room to discuss procedures as far as me releasing him to the state since there would be an automatic investigation because of the circumstances. Finally, we were told we could see him. However, since there would be a required autopsy, they said they couldn't take any equipment off of him, and there were a few reasons his appearance would look different. Ultimately I decided against seeing him then, which was a difficult decision. I wanted to run to him, to hold him, to lie next to him one last time. I also didn't want to see anything that would be difficult to get out of my mind. So, I went with what my heart felt was right. This was my first tough decision to make as a widow (I hate that word). As soon as that decision was made and papers were signed releasing my husband, it was time to get home to our children. Chris' sister Noel and her husband would take me, my brother Brian, and my dad back to our house.

As we rode home from the hospital, I vividly remember asking my dad, "How do I tell the kids?" I dreaded it so badly. And there wasn't an answer for the right thing to say. How could I possibly prepare myself for a moment of this magnitude? Twenty minutes just wasn't enough time. Not for this. I wanted to put it off for as long as possible. The next words I spoke were, "They will not lose their mother too." I vowed in that moment to myself and to them that I would be as close to normal as possible. I was so heartbroken for myself, and for them losing him, yet I was determined to give them as much of me as possible. Of course I would never be the same, but I decided I would be a better mom and I would cherish the moments with them more than I had. I would appreciate them more — their messes, their dirty laundry, and even dirt tracks on the floors because they were still here with me to make them. No matter the pain that I knew was in my future, I vowed to give them smiles and laughs, singing and dancing, craziness and fun. My goal was clear in my mind — to make their lives as meaningful and blessed and joyful as possible, to do everything in my power for them to see their mom, their only Earthly parent now, as a woman of joy, peace, love, comfort and hope. A woman of strength. A woman of faith. A woman of God. That was one of the most significant and defining choices I made immediately. Wisdom was already being placed on my heart without me consciously asking for it.

We arrived home from the hospital with hopeful children anxiously awaiting news about their daddy. My precious mother had been with them a few hours, trying to avoid questions and holding back her own grief to keep them from knowing until I could get to them. As I walked into our house that was still filled with hope and optimism, I had no idea what I would say. My entire trust was placed in Him.

I told the three of them that I needed to talk to them in the bedroom, closed the door behind us, and asked them to climb onto the bed with me. There were questions and doubts swirling through my mind. *How could I pull out enough strength to say the most feared news in their minds? What was I going to say? How could the worst message ever given to them come from their mom?* I've never feared spoken words more than in this moment. I began to pray and depend on the Lord at this point to speak for me. Until now, our babies had hope. Their hearts and spirits had been shielded from the truth until now. It was my responsibility to relay the most life-altering news their little hearts would ever be told, to say the words that would break their spirits, send them into complete shock, and shake the foundation of their security. I certainly didn't want to be this messenger, yet I wanted no one to do it but me.

I finally attempted to look in their frightened little eyes and began speaking the scariest words of my life to our children. I was careful of every syllable I used. There is nothing that can prepare you for this moment. No parenting manual guide instructs you on how to tell your kids their daddy is gone. I was relying on God to show or tell me the way, His way, to guide me in this. And somehow through the shock, panic, and indescribable heartache, I heard so loudly in my mind, *be sure they don't get angry at God*. I felt led. Besides comforting them, that was my focus in choosing my words.

Through raw and utter pain, I explained that daddy was hurt too badly and that he wouldn't be coming home to us. It felt like such a dream. Or like we were now starring in some film that we wanted no part of. I was saying these words, looking at three beautiful children that Chris and I brought into the world, and I couldn't even believe myself. The words were coming out, and I was denying it in my head. I witnessed hope transform to grief in a moment of seconds. Three children shifted from having the perfect family to losing half their security, right before my eyes. The words were spoken, and our innocent, unscarred, and happy-go-lucky kids immediately became overwhelmed with the most enormous loss that would challenge them in ways most adults can't handle well.

I looked in those three sets of teary, heartbroken eyes and told them, "We are going to get through this with God's help. He does not want us to hurt. We are not going to get angry at God that this happened. If there is any anger, it will be directed towards

Satan, who wants us to hurt." I felt I had to immediately be sure they didn't blame the Lord for this tragedy. Of course He was in control and allowed it, for a greater amazing purpose that is so difficult for us to humanly understand. I wanted them to focus on that from the beginning and not get overcome with anger.

Averee, Brody, and Lilly were like their mother, in complete shock. I can't imagine the thoughts that were going through their minds. As twelve, eight, and six year olds, they were processing it the best way they knew how. They didn't know how to react, how to accept, or what to believe. But after the initial shock of the news that night, they calmed down enough for bed. It was late by then, maybe midnight or so. My parents decided to stay with us. I welcomed them to. I knew I wasn't emotionally capable of taking care of myself and three kids at the time.

Brody slept on the large sofa with my dad, my mom slept with Averee, and Lilly slept with me. The kids rested, and I cried almost all night. I kept looking over from my side of the bed to his. I just kept hoping I would see his strong shoulders resting there with his precious head on the pillow, to hear him breathing next to me. I needed with my entire being to just roll over and lay in his arms, to know it was all a horrific dream and that all was good in our world again. But moment by moment reality would not let me escape, constantly reminding me that he would never sleep with me again. I would never look over and see my best friend resting up to be the amazing husband and provider he could be the next morning. I have never felt so hopeless. So vulnerable. So alone. So lost. Many nights I had spent in our bed without him when he would be working all night or out of town. Yet I always knew it was temporary and that he would return to me. That there would be more nights with him there. But now, there would be no more nights because I knew he couldn't return this time. My hope for that was lost. And so I prayed. And sobbed.

"When you pass through the waters, I will be with you; and through the rivers, they shall not overwhelm you; when you walk through fire you shall not be burned, and the flame shall not consume you."

–Isaiah 43:2

"Fear not, for I am with you; be not dismayed, for I am your God; I will strengthen you, I will help you, I will uphold you with my righteous right hand."

–Isaiah 41:10

"I can do all things through Him who strengthens me."

–Philippians 4:13

Chapter 3

NEW MORNING, NEW WORLD

Morning. Waking up and rising from a time of rest with optimism and refreshed hope for new opportunities and unpredictable adventures. A new day dawning to make everything better than the previous one. To praise God for His blessings and our health to face another Earthly day. The rising sun is a symbol of goodness and warmth and peace, a promise of new beginnings His grace provides, a reminder of God's love and comfort and light encouraging and motivating us to embrace the plans He has in store for us.

My first morning without Chris was faced with none of those thoughts. Instead thoughts of uncertainty, fear, and anxiety consumed me. Through the shock and numbness, the sun hurt as much as the dark. The brightness alone reminded me that it indeed wasn't a nightmare. Life would continue, the sun would continue to rise, and so would I. Every day. Without Chris. And questions upon questions began running through my mind: *Yes, I survived the night without him, but how was I supposed to face an entire day? How could I possibly do this and how could the kids live without their daddy? And how did the accident happen? Why did Chris have to go work last night? Is this really what God wants for our lives? Why? What did I do to deserve to lose my husband? Why did our kids have to lose their daddy? Of all the bad people in the world, why him?* There were so many questions. So many decisions to dread. So many fears. And as guilty as it made me feel, another worry hit me quickly—money—and then anger that I was worrying about finances. I tried not to let fear take control, but it sure does like to attack at our weakest moments. And Satan uses it well. Thankfully my parents were there to keep me calm and assure me that the kids and I would be taken care of, no matter what.

I got in the shower that morning, feeling it might help refresh my spirit some. It was the longest amount of time I had been alone since before the accident. What I expected to make me feel better did the complete opposite. Too much sadness awaited me there. There was no one else present to be strong for, no one but me and the harsh reality that would not leave. That couldn't be washed away. I was overwhelmed.

Sorrow began to consume my entire being, and I fell apart right there as that hot water showered down on my weak and vulnerable self. I felt more alone and hopeless than my soul had ever experienced. And in that moment of weakness, I unexpectedly felt my pain shifting to anger. At first I wanted to welcome it, to overcome the sorrow and use my emotion to blame someone and get the focus off myself. But my God, He was stronger. I believe the Spirit led me to tell the kids not to get angry at Him, and the Lord was leading me with the same message. *Don't get angry and don't blame Me. I don't want you to hurt. Reach for the light and fight the dark with the strength that I am giving you.*

I used the only form of defense I knew to use. I immediately said out loud, "Satan, get away from me. Get away from me and my family. You are not going to use this to bring our family down. It won't happen. Get away from me." I have never in my life spoken out loud to the Evil One, but I knew in that moment that it had to be done and the words just came out. I was convinced that he would use every weapon he could against me, and I was going to fight with all the strength I had, the strength that I was certain was only coming from the Father.

So I told Satan to shut up, and I began to cling to hope and the comfort of knowing where my sweet, saved husband was spending his morning. *Paradise.* Yes. That one thought alone. It was the place I found peace and comfort and strength and hope. I just had to place my mind on what Chris was experiencing. *Heaven.* The name alone is majestic. It's overwhelming to try and imagine. Our forever home. When I shifted my mind to eternity, with Heaven as my focus, my spirit calmed and the fear subsided. Of course it didn't take away the pain of grief, but it sent some relief over me. *How could I think of Chris in Heaven and be sad about that? And how could I be angry when he had received his reward? As Christians our goal in life is eternity with our Lord, and Chris had made it!* I had all the faith in the world that he was with our Heavenly Father. I knew the knowledge of that would help me overcome the fear and pain. It was the only thing that could. My faith would be my armor and protect me from the darkness. Besides just surviving this storm, my new goal was to defeat Satan every minute of every hour of every day from this day forward. I never really knew just how strong a shield my faith was. It had never really been tested. Until now.

We spent that first morning trying to figure out what decisions to make and when to do what. I called the pool contractor first thing that morning to let him know whatever the consequences, I couldn't have a pool being built in our back yard. It would have to be postponed until maybe next year. He was understanding.

That Friday was filled with family and friends and Chris' co-workers bringing sympathy and hugs and food and gifts and sharing memories and tears with us. Part of me wanted to run screaming down the driveway as far as I could possibly go and pretend it wasn't happening. Or maybe just go lock myself in my bedroom with the covers over my head and block it all out. Forever. But I didn't. There were three little souls watching my every move and if they ever needed their mother, it was now. Even if I were in tears most of the time, I was there with them and they knew we were fighting the pain together.

A lot of that day is a blur to me now, I guess because I was just surviving moment by moment, and my mind was spinning so much I had difficulty processing the truth, much less being able to store a memory. I do remember, though, that Friday night going to bed, this time with the decision to lay down on Chris' side. I had decided that it was the only way I couldn't look to his vacant side anymore because I would be sleeping on it. Again, survival.

Saturday rolled around after an exhausting day and another long night. I rested some thankfully. In this day awaited decisions that I wanted so badly to ignore. I was struggling with wanting to keep procrastinating and not making these decisions and wanting everything to be perfect since I knew there was no safety button to help me escape this reality. First decision: choosing from the closet the last outfit Chris would ever wear. Goodness, I was used to picking out his clothes. Most of the time on Sunday mornings he would ask me to pick him out something to wear. I'm not sure if he thought I had better taste than him or he just liked being taken care of in that way. I never asked because I liked taking care of him. And here I found myself, for the final time, hand-picking a button up and khakis and belt for my beloved Chris. I was heartbroken and honored at the same time. That was a combination I would get accustomed to feeling over time. My mom offered to iron the clothes for me, but I wouldn't have dared missed the opportunity to get his clothes ready for him one last time.

Next came the trip to the funeral home to plan his service. Beyond exhaustion and pain I had to decide the way to honor and memorialize my husband, who had not even been gone for two days yet. Chris and I had never talked about these sort of plans. We took out life insurance and planned on living until we were at least senior citizens. Oh, and we knew we had burial plots at the cemetery of the church his mother grew up in. With everything else I did the only thing I knew to do. Pray for strength, think of what Chris would want, and get through it. It was long and difficult, and I had all our parents there to help decide and give input. I wanted them involved. I knew what had helped my parents get through the loss of my brother, and I decided to let Chris' parents be as big a part as they were capable of handling. I tried from the beginning to always take their feelings into consideration and do whatever I could to help them cope.

We decided to spend the next morning with our immediate family being able to see him. We knew we needed a separate day for that. Then we would do the visitation and service on Monday. His service would be at the church he was baptized in and spent a great deal of his life, and he would be buried at the other church he spent a lot of his life. That seemed perfect to me.

We finally made it back home later in the afternoon to lots more family and friends and the kids who had been occupied by cousins playing in the yard a lot of the day. I was so thankful for that. They needed distractions and busyness and fun.

Some of Chris' co-workers had come out to cut our grass, and I was so appreciative and impressed by that. Those men were already showing me how much they cared, how helpless they felt, the love and respect they had for Chris. They needed to do something. Anything. To put their pain into an act of kindness for his family. Out of all the blurred memories of that time, them doing that is forever clearly engraved in my heart and mind.

There is much from these first days following Chris' accident that is a complete blur, and then a lot that is crystal clear. I believe God has a purpose in that. I remember the uncontrollable shock and grief, the pure exhaustion of it all, and that it seemed like I was watching some horrific film of my life of which I couldn't change the plot or script. I had gone from wife to widow without warning, held hostage in acting out this new role. In this exhausted state, I know God was covering me and guiding me with such difficult decisions. I have thought since *how in the world did I get through that?* And then it's like God hits me upside the head. *With me!* I believe the Holy Spirit was filling me up and carrying me through the motions. I was too out of myself to even think to pray enough on my own. Thank the Lord He knew my heart and helped me anyway.

I spent Saturday night pretty much locked in my bedroom going through every picture in my possession of Chris and our family. A dear friend of mine was going to do a slideshow to be played at his memorial service, and with all the visitors we had it was difficult to find time to do it. It doesn't seem like that huge of a job. But deciding how to visibly represent a man's entire life into a few minutes of photos is, well, an enormous task, especially when the man is the love of your life and the father of your children.

It seemed that all other decisions were incredibly difficult as well. Deciding who would be pallbearers was one of those. Chris had a multitude of friends and family and co-workers and for me to try and decide how to narrow it down stressed me out more than I should have let it. I was worrying about people's feelings and everything else under the sun. But I got it done. I decided on his closest friends and co-workers at the time. And the Florence Electricity Department guys would be honorary pallbearers. I couldn't leave a single one of them out of the honor. They would have all carried him if they could.

Then there were music selections. Goodness, no one anticipates all the decisions to make during the most difficult of circumstances, and my brain was overcome with trying to accept the reality that was bringing about these decisions. God provided in His own way. I immediately thought of the song "I Can Only Imagine." The song has always made me smile and cry at the same time. With thoughts of Chris experiencing the words in this song, my heart was overwhelmed. The lyrics uplifted me with hope and faith of our reward in Heaven.

"Ten Thousand Reasons" was the next song laid upon my heart. It was a song so dear to our family. Chris would sing it out if it came on the radio or at church. He and Lilly sang the words several times sitting together in our big comfy chair. This beautiful song was a given. It was exactly what my heart felt and yearned to continue to feel towards the Lord. It had to be included. Such a powerful message and the memories behind it made it even more precious.

On Saturday morning when I was ironing Chris' clothes, Lilly had come into the bedroom with me. I said, "Hey Lilly, guess what song I was thinking we should play at Daddy's service?" She immediately said, "I know what song, 'See You Again.' The Carrie Underwood song." It was as though she was certain that's the one I would have picked. And so I told her about "Ten Thousand Reasons" and that I felt that song was perfect as well. I told her I would think about including it, and later when I had time alone to listen to the words, I sobbed with grief and was renewed with hope from the lyrics.

When we went to the funeral home to make the service arrangements, Chris' mom had mentioned that she would love it if a Garth Brooks song was included somehow. When Chris was in high school everyone said he looked like Garth with his western style clothes and cowboy boots. Being honest, when she mentioned playing one of his songs, I wasn't quite sure it would be appropriate. And then that Saturday night when my dad and I were in the living room with Brody talking about songs, I listened to "The Dance." How perfect of a song. Another beautiful message.

After listening to "The Dance" that night, I asked Brody if he had any ideas and he said, "You know the song by Darryl Worley, 'I Miss My Friend.' I think it would be a good one." He remembered watching the music video with me and Chris before. We listened to it together and my dad and I looked at each other through tears. Yes. It had to be played as well. It was a song that completely described my feelings as his wife.

As much as I felt overwhelmed and inadequate to make the massive amount of painful decisions at the time, God was providing me with the assistance and knowledge and comfort with everything being decided. That night, with the dread of the next couple of days weighing down on my heart, my soul felt peace with what had come together in planning our goodbye and celebration of Chris. There was no peace over the goodbye itself, but the celebration of his life and now his eternity. I had to keep my mind on his Heavenly home. It was the only way I was getting through. Complete and unwavering faith.

Before we went to bed this night, the night before we would see Chris for the first time since he left our home June 5th, I had a visit from my children in the bedroom that was of great magnitude in my memory. Averee was obviously the leader of it, but Brody and Lilly were proudly there alongside her. Here they came with smiles across their faces, carrying a big plate full of goodies they had gathered to deliver to me. I had to force happiness in seeing food, as my stomach turned at the idea of eating. I didn't have to force happiness in their caring hearts. The realization that they, in all their pain and adjustment, were taking care of their mother, filled my heart with pride for the amazingly strong and compassionate babies Chris and I had raised together.

I also learned in that moment how observant kids are to how you react and deal with tragic situations because I had barely eaten since Thursday night. When I say barely, I mean the day after I only ate a few bites of bread all day, and I had to force it down. The thought of food made me extremely nauseous.

Averee had mentioned to her youth minister Joe (a close friend of ours) that she was worried about me because I wasn't eating. I was honestly shocked when he told me. We had so many waves of people coming in and out of our house, and the kids were running around so much. I never dreamed they would have been watching. I was wrong.

I decided I had to take care of myself physically even though there was a loss of self-control somewhat emotionally. And I had to be sure the kids saw me taking care of myself. I had to be sure they knew I was going to be ok. They did not need the worry or fear of my well-being. I couldn't take care of them if I wasn't well, and they knew that. They needed me.

On this night as my head hit the pillow, I prayed for God to just let me be able to eat some and keep my strength up physically and of course emotionally. I tried to mentally prepare my soul for the next morning. Seeing Chris. The kids seeing Chris. For the tangible evidence of his passing being right in front of our eyes. I didn't know how to prepare. So I prayed. A lot. I don't remember my exact words to God, but I remember using these phrases a lot those first few days:

Dear Lord, give me strength. Wrap Your arms around me and the kids and just carry us through this. I can't do this without You, Lord. Just fill me up with Your presence and help me through it. Use me for good, Lord. Let good come from this. I can't handle just darkness and pain. Give me light, Lord. Let Chris' life be a testimony for You, Lord. No matter what, I trust You and Your plan for my life. I know You love me, Father. Your will be done.

"Then you will call upon me and come and pray to me, and I will hear you. You will seek me and find me with all your heart."

–Jeremiah 29:12-13

"The light shines in the darkness, and the darkness has not overcome it."

–John 1:5

"Blessed be the Lord! For He has heard the voice of my pleas for mercy. The Lord is my strength and my shield; in Him my heart trusts, and I am helped;"

–Psalm 28:6-7

Chapter 4

I'LL SEE YOU AGAIN

Sunday, June 8, 2014.

Our Sunday mornings had always consisted of getting up, dressing in our best and heading out as a family to worship the Lord and learn more about Him and His amazing grace. It was such a constant every week in the midst of sometimes going in so many different directions. No matter what, we always had Sunday to bring our family together with a common goal.

On this hot, summer Alabama Sunday, we indeed got up. We dressed in our best. And although we prepared to head into town as a family, our family looked completely different now. It looked unbalanced. Incomplete. Wrong. The void was overwhelming.

This Sunday would not include worship and praise for the Williamsons. It would look different than any we had ever experienced. There was a common goal, and our family would be brought together but not by desire or choice.

We knew we needed a separate day before the service to see Chris and spend time with him before we had to face others. But oh, how we dreaded it! How we wanted to stay in the depths of the

67

dream state and not have to deal with the reality we knew would hit. Brody said he did not want to go. He meant it. He really didn't. I told him he had to go to the funeral home, but if it was too difficult I wouldn't make him go in to see his daddy. I felt he needed to feel somewhat in control since everything else felt so much out of it. And I knew Brody would decide to do what he needed for his heart.

Chris and I didn't realize what strong kids we were raising. Super strong. I pray every day for their strength and positive outlook. However, like me, they were forced into roles they didn't ask for and certainly didn't want. They didn't know how to be children without a daddy, and I certainly couldn't tell them how to do it the *right* way. We were just figuring it out as we went through it.

After arriving at the funeral home that morning and meeting immediate family I had asked to come, it was time to go upstairs and see him.

Chris' parents and I went in first, me between them with locked arms. It would have been beautiful had it not been so excruciating—the three of us walking into that parlor room towards a man who God had gifted us with for thirty-nine short but oh so significant years. The man who made Gary and Kay parents. Who first gave them the feeling of unconditional love. The man who was once their little boy. Who would always be their little boy. Their son. Their baby. One who had brought so much joy into their lives. And for me, the man who made me an extremely happy wife. The man who stole my heart and took care of me and helped me bring three beautiful children into the world. Who always worked so hard and put his family first in all ways. Who I had planned to grow old with. My husband. My protector. And provider. Comforter. Best friend. Lover. My other half in every way. Literally.

Uncontrollable pain does not describe it. Neither does shock and dismay. A description of feeling simply does not exist for that moment. There was lots of courage though. And strength. As we approached his beautiful earthly body, so handsome and strong, lying in a beautiful, stained, wooden bed with a spread of all white roses and lilies lying atop.

For three long days I had yearned to see him: his face, his broad shoulders and hard-working hands, those incredibly long eyelashes that I had always been so jealous of. I had been constantly waiting and looking to see him among the crowds of people that had been at our home. I found myself waiting for him to come through the door, to end this charade and get us back to our incredible life. My mind had not completely taken hold of the truth. Until now.

This was the moment when the nightmare became an undeniable reality. Seeing him like I had so desperately wanted but in a completely different way. Obviously, I had been told my husband passed away, and I believed it to be true, but to see his lifeless body for the first time, well, my heart has never felt so broken. From the second my eyes could focus enough through tears upon entering that room, I knew. Beyond a shadow of a doubt. Chris was in Heaven now. I was here, with our three beautiful children, children he had planned on being here for while they grew up, graduated school, got married, had babies. Chris would never have chosen to leave us. But here we were, caught in this sharp turn going in a completely different direction than our plan. I hated this path. However, spiritually I knew that *our plan* wasn't God's plan, and now, well I had to allow trust to guide me through.

The three of us stood there for a while, doing the only thing we could. We held each other up and sobbed.

There is such an understanding—a realization—when you see a loved one whose spirit has made the transition into eternity. We looked at Chris, washed our souls with tears, and shared memories. And I think once we made it through the initial shock of this horrific truth for us, we internalized the truth that Chris wasn't there. We were looking at what had been the home of his magnificent spirit. Of course that did not ease our pain and desire for him to come back. The mourning was stronger than ever. But next to the grief, I felt peace begin to wash over me and fill my fragile spirit, knowing he had only moved to his new home, his real home. And that although we now couldn't see him, he still existed—just out of reach temporarily. At least for me, that was where my hope lived: in seeing him again one day. Once again my faith took charge. I knew with complete certainty where this sweet man's spirit now resided, and I knew the Lord would see us through being here without him.

Our immediate family came in next. I decided to let everyone else get through this painful moment before bringing the kids up. I dreaded bringing them up. But once everyone else had calmed down enough to be able to support the kids in the best way, it was time. Brody still said on the way upstairs that he wasn't going into the room, and I didn't push him. My dad and brother stood in the hall with him and I said, "Ok son, well you can tell Paw Paw if you decide you can come in." My courageous girls came in with me, and it was probably ten minutes of him standing at the door looking in until he finally decided it was time. My boy was so brave as I walked him in. I knew exactly how he felt, but I knew he needed the closure. Regardless, I decided he needed to be able to make the decision of what he could handle.

There was more pride and admiration for our children that day than I had ever experienced. What they were battling and how they were handling themselves, they conquered life that day as far as I was concerned.

We spent a few hours in the parlor room with Chris' body, admiring him and sharing tears, embraces, and sweet memories. After the initial shock of reality and spending some time there, we were able to just sit and visit and take turns walking back up and spending time with him. It was incredibly helpful and healing to just let reality soak into our souls.

Although I say reality took residence in my heart this day, it's still amazing how vastly surreal the experience was, which is completely contradictory. Grief doesn't follow the rules. You can feel two opposite truths and emotions at the same time and somehow make sense of it. I continued to feel I was in a bad dream through all of it. Seeing Averee, Brody, and Lilly stand next to their daddy, touching him and processing it all, their little souls experiencing more than I could fathom, was a picture of magnitude that can't be expressed in words.

At one moment, as I was sitting in a chair in the room, Lilly walked back to me after looking at her daddy. She climbed in my lap, held my cheeks with her little hands, and whispered in my ear. "Daddy is giving me a message in my mind." I said, "What's he saying, baby?" She said, "He's singing 'You Are My Sunshine.'" I asked her how that made her feel. She said it made her feel good. That's all that mattered. The fact is he never sang that to her. But one month earlier, she was the sunshine in her kindergarten play. I believed what that baby girl said to be absolutely true then, and I still do.

After spending several hours in that room with Chris, we left to go home and attempt to rest before the next day, which we knew would be exhausting beyond our imagination. We arrived to our house with lots of food and family and friends, which was a blessing once again. As much as I didn't want to socialize with anyone, all of us needed that love around us.

We made it through one of the most difficult days that day. We were in somewhat of a fog and things seemed very blurry a lot of the time, but the constant through it all was me feeling God's presence with us. His signs and promises were clear and very visible. It was the one truth that I knew wouldn't be shaken. I had this proof once again of how fragile our Earthly bodies are and what a vapor this life is, and my spirit was drawn to Heaven more than it had ever been. As I lay down that Sunday night mentally and physically drained, I was focused on praying with all my might for God's presence to stay loud and clear through the next day, which would be more of a challenge. There's no way to mentally prepare for laying your husband to rest. You ask God to strengthen you, you ask God to give you peace, and you ask God to hold you up if needed and carry you through it. And that's exactly what I did that night.

"Hear my cry, O God, listen to my prayer; from the end of the earth I call to you when my heart is faint. Lead me to the rock that is higher than I."

–Psalm 61:1-2

"Do not be anxious about anything, but in everything by prayer and supplication with thanksgiving let your requests be made known to God. And the peace of God, which surpasses all understanding, will guard your hearts and minds in Christ Jesus."

–Philippians 4:6-7

"Trust in the Lord with all your heart, and do not lean on your own understanding. In all your ways acknowledge Him, and He will make straight your paths."

–Proverbs 3:5-6

Chapter 5

BLESS THE LORD,
OH MY SOUL

Monday, June 9th.

Another extremely challenging day awaited us as we rose and began to get dressed for Chris' service. My parents were still with us, which was a blessing. I needed to feel as if I were being looked after and taken care of somewhat.

Everything still seemed surreal in many ways. Thinking about what the day would entail, the dread was all consuming. The finality in what we were facing was more than my soul knew how to bear. But again, I filled my mind and spirit with constant prayer and positive thoughts. I was convinced it was the only way I could make it through the day, and beyond.

We arrived at Jackson Heights Church of Christ around 9:15 that morning. My dad drove us. The eight pallbearers I had chosen to honor Chris were there, along with our immediate family and several of his co-workers. We spent some time embracing, crying and sharing memories, and preparing mentally before visitation, which started at 10:00. I also spent some time with the kids looking at their daddy and helping comfort them and prepare them for what we would be experiencing through the day.

I gave the kids some power on what they could handle. I had decided Chris' casket would be open for viewing, but I told the three of them they didn't have to be in the auditorium during the visitation if it was too difficult. I knew it would be too much for them for four hours. Some friends had brought food and set it up in a classroom at the church for the kids to go to as a sort of escape.

Ten o'clock came with an enormous amount of friends and family who had been waiting outside: a never-ending line of love and support, tears and hugs, memories and funny stories, and of course mourning and grief. But mostly, Chris' life was represented by every individual who stood in line for hours upon hours to tell me what his presence meant to them and how he impacted their lives. It was more clear than ever to me. The massive amount of respect and love for my husband filled up that gigantic space. Chris could never have imagined how much he was loved. And admired. And looked up to. He could never have imagined how devastated people would be that they would never hear his amazing laugh again or hear him cheer at one of the kids' ballgames, to see that wonderful smile and see the light in his beautiful hazel eyes. They would never call a turkey with him or ride in a bucket truck by his side or talk to him through an all-nighter at work. I witnessed so much pain from so many who were aching with the same feelings I had. Helplessness. Emptiness. Despair. Feeling the void of this amazing individual who had blessed their lives in so many different but incredible ways.

I met some I didn't know, even some Chris didn't know. There were men from other local electricity departments who came to show respect for a man they had never met but were bonded to by their brotherhood. There were childhood friends of Chris and a multitude of members of our community and church and schools he and I attended and some people I would have never expected to come honestly. Yet they were there, every special person in our lives. So many in fact, we couldn't get them all through the line by two o'clock. It was extremely difficult for me to agree to let them cut the line off so that we could begin the service. The director told me that we would be short on time for the service and burial if we didn't. So we apologized and did what we needed to do. I didn't know at the time there were many who couldn't even get into the auditorium to sit down as the entire space was already filled.

A little after two o'clock. I looked at my husband's face and touched him for the last time this side of eternity. I leaned over his beautiful body and kissed him and sobbed. I tried to not think about the fact that it was the last time we would touch. In fact, I tried to not think the words *last time*. They crushed me too much.

Our immediate family gathered in a small room while the director removed Chris' wedding band for me and they prepared for the service. Inside Chris' casket with him was a teddy bear Lilly had placed with the year of her birth embroidered on it, a Boston Red Sox baseball cap that Brody had placed inside (he and his daddy's favorite baseball team), and a softball Averee felt was perfect in honor of all of the many hours they spent together practicing the sport.

"Ten Thousand Reasons" began playing over the speakers as we came back into the auditorium and took our seats in the church. We then listened to "I Miss My Friend." Afterwards, Ronnie Pannell, a lifelong mentor of Chris and friend of the Williamson family, took his place at the podium to begin the memorial service. His words were as follows:

"Let not your heart be troubled: You believe in God, believe also in me. In my Father's house are many mansions: If it were not so I would have told you. I go to prepare a place for you. And if I go and prepare a place for you, I will come again, and receive you unto myself; that where I am, there ye may be also. And whither I go ye know and the way ye know. Thomas said unto him, 'Lord, we know not whither thou goest; and how can we know the way?' Jesus said unto him, 'I am the way, the truth, and the life: No man comes to the Father but by me.'" (John 14:1-6)

We gather today to remember the life of Christopher Lane Williamson. To show our love to his family. To share stories of how this family member and this friend impacted our lives. To remember how Chris was a blessing to each of us. He was a friend. He was a loving husband, a father, a son, brother, uncle, grandson. To those of you who think about working alongside him every day, to those of you who attended Cross Point Church of Christ with him, and to those who have seen him at Mars Hill Bible School supporting his children and activities they were involved in.

Christopher Lane Williamson departed this life

June 5, 2014 at the age of thirty-nine. His survivors are his wife Andrea Williamson, children Averee Faith, Brody Lane and Lilly Grace Williamson; parents Kay Angel Danley (husband Ricky), Gary Williamson (wife Tammra); grandmothers Margaret Angel and Margaret Williamson; siblings Noel Staggs (husband Jeremy), Heather Robertson (husband Heath), Billy Williamson; nephews Issac Staggs and Case Robertson; mother and father-in-law Rufus and Sharon Johnson; grandmother-in-law Wynoka Irons.

The scene Thursday night at ECM was very difficult. Everyone that was there cared. That's why they were there. And everyone down there wanted to do something to change it. Every one of us wanted to somehow fix it. And we couldn't. It's so hard seeing people hurt.

I left the Florence Gas Department the summer of 1987 after working there ten years. I came here to Jackson Heights as the associate minister and the youth minister. By November I had baptized five young people. One of them was Chris Williamson. Another one was Les Abston. And Jon Pannell sitting in the balcony.

I think about Chris. The connections that he had. First of all his family. And then he had a Jackson Heights family as he grew up. And then Wilson High School. Florence Electricity Department. Cross Point Church of Christ. Mars Hill Bible School. But his number one family—his loving wife and three wonderful children.

I do want to take a moment to talk to the city of Florence employees. Thank you. Thank you for what you do for our community. To every employee from the decision makers to the crews. It's been a long time ago that I've been there. I've seen first hand some of the things that you're asked to do. When everyone else is headed for safety, you're headed for danger. Same can be said for our Police Department, Fire Department, other departments in the city. So many times through the years, citizens of Florence and of Lauderdale County have watched as your trucks roll into the storm areas, to put your lives in harms way, so we can have electricity. Sit in our comfortable recliners and watch our televisions, be cool by our air conditioners, be warm by our heaters, while you employees, you're fighting the elements to allow us to have comfort. Thank you and may God bless you in what you do. I hope that we as citizens of Florence will have more appreciation for what you do for us and we'll realize the risk that you take on our behalf. How unfortunate it is that it takes a tragedy like this for us to realize what's really important!

Mickey Haddock called Chris a bright star within the department. I agree, mayor. Matthew chapter five and verse sixteen says, "Let your light so shine before men that they may see your good works, and glorify your Father which is in Heaven." Chris was a light. He was a light to all of us. It was always a joy to see Chris. Maybe he was up to no good but when you would see him, you would start smiling. His personality, that smile, his laughter. His ability to care and to share. To share his time. The coaching he did and the things he did to help others, at school, church and in the community. He gave of himself. He was a team player.

It's been said death leaves a heartache that no one can heal, but love leaves a memory that no one can steal.

I ran across this story: One recent summer a bee was drawn into the open window of a car driving down the road. The bee was upset and so was the boy in the car, who had previously suffered a severe reaction from a bee sting. But before things got out of hand, the boy's father caught the bee in his hand and tossed it out the window. Then he pulled the car over to comfort his son. The boy was now desperately worried that his father would die from the bee sting. "Oh no," said the father, showing him his hand was only lightly swollen. "The sting won't hurt me like it would you. So I took the sting for you."

And that's what Jesus did for us. He took the sting of death for us and now that sting is gone. First Corinthians chapter fifteen beginning in verse fifty-five: "O death where is thy sting? O grave where is thy victory? The sting of death is sin...But thanks be to God, which giveth us the victory through our Lord Jesus Christ." Proverbs chapter three says, "Trust in the Lord with all thine heart; and lean not unto thine own understanding. In all thy ways acknowledge Him, and He shall direct thy paths." Proverbs ten and verse seven says the memory of a good person is a blessing.

Many of you have wondered what to do for this family. Well, first of all being here. I'm reminded of Job. There are a lot of lessons in the book of Job. To me one of the strongest ones comes in the second chapter when his three friends join him. And you need to read carefully and understand what went on. It says that for seven days and seven nights they sat with him and did not speak a word. So when you're looking for the right word to say, that's really not the most important thing. Just be there. Being here today, being there Thursday night, being with the family over the last few days. When you see people come in, you know they care about you. That's very important.

What can you do? One thing that we need to do is to understand that for this family, there is a new normal. Things will never be the same. They can't be. You need to do your best to understand this. And unless you've been there, you just can't understand. You gotta learn to be patient. You gotta give hugs and handshakes and pats on the back. A card, give to a charity or some cause in Chris' memory. Don't be scared to mention Chris to this family. They will want to talk about him. They'll want to share stories. And they want to laugh. And they want to cry. And it's ok. If you want to say something, tell them you love them. Tell them you care about them. Tell them that you're going to pray for them. But make sure you keep your word.

Andrea, on behalf of Mr. Dexter Rutherford, president of Mars Hill Bible School, I commit to you that the faculty and staff at Mars Hill Bible School will do everything that we possibly can to help you take care of your children. Whatever you need, you let us know.

Siblings, please remember the fondness. All the happy times. You've got to hold onto the happy times. Billy, you got to celebrate a state championship with Chris. How special!

Kay and Ricky, Gary and Tammra. I want to share a story with you that has helped Kathy and me over the last nine years. An older lady left Buffalo by boat for Cleveland to visit a daughter living there. And soon a dreadful storm came up and many of the passengers who were scared gathered for prayer. Only the older lady seemed unconcerned as she sat with her hands folded and she prayed. After the storm subsided some of the passengers were eager to know the secret of her calmness. They gathered around and asked her the reason. "Well, my dear friends," she replied. "It's like this. I have two daughters. One died and went home to Heaven. The other lives in Cleveland. When the storm arose, I wondered which I might visit first. The one in Cleveland, or the one in Heaven. And I just left it to the Lord. For I would be glad to see either one."

May Almighty God grant unto you peace and comfort and strength. Good memories of Chris. And the assurance of being together one day for eternity in Heaven. And as I've mentioned and no doubt Frank will be mentioning, the fact of all you friends and what you've done. And on behalf of this wonderful family, I want to thank you for any and every act of kindness and love that's been shown this week.

I love y'all. You're a special family. And that doesn't change now. You're still a very very special family. Thank you for allowing me to be a part of this service. Chris was a wonderful person to be around, and he will be missed.

Would you bow with me for prayer?

Our heavenly Father, it's with heavy hearts that we come to You today. As we are saddened and going to miss our friend Chris here. But, Father, we live our lives with the promise that You've given us of an eternity together with those that love You and serve You. And even though we know that and we understand that, it still is hard at this point in time. Father, please give this family strength and comfort. Give them some understanding. Give them patience. Give them guidance. We ask You to bless Andrea and Averee and Brody and Lilly. We ask You to bless the entire family. Father, help us to see how we can help them. Help us be willing to do those things necessary. Father, we do thank You for this community, and we thank You for the people who work to make our community so good. We do thank You for the city of Florence and the employees there. How decisions are made to make this community better. And then when storms do come along, when bad times come along, we have men and women who will respond and who will help us and take care of us. We thank You for them. And we ask You, Father, to bless them, to keep them safe and watch over them. We thank You for them. We thank You for Jesus. We thank You for His life and for His blessings. And His love. And we thank You Father for Your gift of salvation. Thank You for making it possible that we can have that grand reunion one day with all those loved ones who've gone on before, and from then on we'll be together with You. Be with Frank as he delivers his message, Father, and we thank You for Cross Point. We thank You for Jackson Heights. We thank You for the influence of these congregations on this community. And we pray that we always serve You faithfully. Thank You, Father, for loving us. It's in Your Son's name we pray, Amen.

"I Can Only Imagine" played next.

And then our minister at Cross Point, Frank Mills, took the podium.

Thank you, my brother. I know that wasn't

easy. And you honored him well. Thank you very much. The words of the Psalms are soothing and strengthening in times like this when my human words are inadequate. The Psalms, many of which were written by the singers of Israel, and even more by the sweet singer himself, David. He wrote many of his songs and prayers from personal experiences that he had to endure. He lost a son in infancy and had an adult son die, and as brother Ronnie said only those of you who have been in those shoes truly know. But if you wear the term, you know who to lean on. I hope in the language of the apostle Paul that we can find the hope and strength today to continue to press on, as the language of Acts chapter thirteen says to continue to serve God's purposes in our own generation. So, would you listen to the words of the singers of Israel? "God is our refuge and strength. An ever-present help in trouble. Therefore, we will not fear. Though the Earth give way and the mountains fall into the sea, the Lord almighty is with us. The God of Jacob is our fortress. So be still and know that I am God." And from David, "He heals the broken hearted and binds up their wounds. Thou O God are a God of compassion, abounding in grace and mercy and truth. Trust in Him at all times. Pour out your heart to Him. The Lord is my shepherd. Yea though I walk through the shadow of death I will fear no evil for thou art with me." Aren't you grateful that David focused on the shepherd instead of the storm? For his merciful kindness of grace towards us. And the truth of the Lord endures forever. Praise You Lord. That's what we want to do today, so would you bow with me please...

Our Father, who art in Heaven hallowed be thy name. We praise You for blessing our lives with Chris Williamson. And like our Lord's Earthly mother Mary treasured all the things in her heart that had been told to her about her son, it is my prayer that Chris' family will also treasure in their hearts all the wonderful and kind things that were just told to them in the past few hours and in the last few days. We ask in faith that You bring this family and to all of us who were his friends Your comfort and strength not only today, but in the days to come as we go in different directions. May You be glorified in this service and the way that we honor Chris' life and may we all live in such a way that will glorify You and honor his memory in the way that we live in the days to come. It's in the name of Your precious Son that we pray, Amen.

Before I tell you what we're about to do, I want to share a powerful story that's filled with hope from the New Testament. It's found in Luke 7. It's a story that centers on Jesus, the One that came to heal the broken hearted and bind up our wounds and turn our sorrows into joys by conquering death in the grave and sin and Satan, and therefore is the Resurrection and the Life. Jesus had left Capernaum, and a large crowd was following Him. And as they entered into the town of

Nain, a funeral procession was coming down the city. You remember what Jesus did first. He sobbed. Just like you've done on this afternoon. And so on behalf of the family here, I too want to thank you for stopping what you do on a typical Monday afternoon and giving something very precious to this family, which is your time and your presence and your love.

As President Lincoln once said, it is altogether fitting and proper that we do this. He ended that service at that cemetery by saying the world won't know or long remember what we say here, but it must never forget what was done here.

Jesus stopped when He saw that funeral procession. But I believe there was another reason that He stopped. I believe He stopped not because of the crowds but because He saw the look in the eye of that twice-bereaved mother. The Bible says His heart went out to her. And so speaking for all of us here, our hearts go out to you. Jesus said to that twice-bereaved woman, "Don't cry." It's not because there's not a time to do so because the wise man Solomon says, It's ok. But I believe He said don't cry because He knew He was the Resurrection and the Life and what He was about to do. And He brought that boy, and He raised him up and He gave him back to his mother, and the Bible says all of the people praised God. And said God's come to help all His people. So, we're claiming that scripture for you today.

And here's what I want to say and then I'll tell you what I'm gonna do. Our culture tells us that this is the time to pay our last respects to someone we dearly love. Preachers are called to be truth tellers. And so, I say to you today, that's essentially not true. We all respected Chris so much, and we gave him our respect and love while he was here with us, but this is NOT the last time that we will honor his life and pay our respects to him. Because he was a child of God who lived out his faith in the Son of God and lived out the two greatest commands, which are love God with all our hearts, souls, strength and mind and love our neighbor as our self. Because he lived by Micah 6:8, which says one of the things that the Lord requires of us is to "do justly, and to love mercy and to walk humbly with thy God." Because of all of that, this is not the end of life.

I want to quickly do five things this afternoon. We're gonna praise God for blessing our lives and the city and this church and the Cross Point Church and the kingdom and his family with Chris Williamson. At Cross Point we sing, "Blessed be Your name in the land that is plentiful, where your streams of abundance flow, blessed be Your name." It's easy to do that when everything's good, isn't it? But we also sing, "Blessed be Your name on a road marked with suffering, though there's pain in the offering, blessed be Your name."

And we're gonna do that today, and then we're

gonna practice a biblical command in Galatians 6, which tells us to bear each other's burdens and so fulfill the law of Christ. And then I'm gonna share with you some things that I hope will encourage you and honor his life. I'm gonna share then a challenge with you and then we'll close by sharing with you some words that we sang Wednesday night and then one of the most powerful passages in scripture. And if we can do that then we can leave here even more committed than ever to live like we are called to live. And God will be glorified and Christ will be exalted and Chris' life will be honored like it deserves to be honored, and hopefully his family will be strengthened.

So I want to say, Chris Williamson had a smile that would light up a room as big as the Grand Canyon, and if you can close your eyes with me you can almost see it right now. He was upbeat, happy, joyous, full of life, and Jesus said he had come for us to live that way. One of his best friends told me he didn't seem to ever be in a bad mood or have a bad day. Let me just say, Can that be said of you? Or his preacher? That's a mouthful.

The question was once asked, How can you measure a man? I want to try and answer today. You can measure this way. Whether or not that man was a family man, whether he was a man of faith, whether he had his continual heartbeat with God. You can look at his priorities and you can look at his friends. And I want to say something about a few of those.

He was a family man. He loved living way out, what I call way out, on family land. He loved the way he was raised, what he was taught by his Paw, what he was taught by his mother and father, the values they instilled in him. He learned to grow up to enjoy God's creation, to take care of things, to take care of the cows and each other and to give. He was raised right. He always said "yes, sir" and "no, sir" to me. A person who was raised right. He had a lot of love in his life, but the wind beneath his wings was Andrea, and I asked her to tell me about him, and she said he was an awesome husband and he was, he was a great provider. If you read the obituary in the paper, he was. He sacrificed as anyone does to send the three children to Mars Hill, and that's a sacrifice. He was a nurturer. He was one who wanted to take good care of each of you, and he did. And I want to say that you were the perfect complement to him. You were. And I'm so grateful that you guys had the opportunity to go to the beach last week. That time is very, very special.

He was an incredible dad who would come home from a long day of work, having worked a lot of hours and if they wanted to play or pitch or catch, he was up for it and committed to it because his line was, "I am not gonna be one of those dads who never has time."

I asked his three precious children to talk to me

about their dad, and I want to share with you what they said.

From Averee: "He was my number one fan, coach, and wonderful dad. He was also a great role model. I want to tell you this story. It was a stormy night, and my dad and mom and Brody and I were in my parents' bed with the power out. I started feeling scared at the age of four so I said, 'Dad, when will the lights come back on?' He said, 'When I say the magic words. Are you ready? One, two, three, let there be light.' When I heard this I thought there's no way of it happening, but it did! I looked up and said, 'Daddy, you're a magician,' and he smiled. This story has stuck with me for eight years. I've always thought the world of my dad and I always will."

And Brody, where are you? You're a spittin' image of him. Did you guys see the picture of both of them? I mean it was a throwback, wasn't it? And I believe he was excited as you were, my friend, when you got your Nick Saban football. And when you wore your Brody Croyle jersey to football camp at Mars Hill. He was excited. And your preacher was excited when I gave the devo and saw it and when you got your McCarron jersey, your dad was excited as well.

Brody said: "We were playing baseball in the yard one day, and Dad told me to feed the chickens. The feed scoop was in the pen, and Dad said to go in there and get it, so I did. Then the rooster started running towards me, and I started screaming for help. Dad ran down there and said, 'Kick, it Brody!' I started to hit it with the scoop. Its feathers started sticking up around its head. Dad jumped in the pen and told me to get out. Then he bent down and said to the rooster, 'You want a piece of me?!' That rooster flew towards Dad, and he kicked the thing across the pen. Boom!" Isn't that great?

And this is what Lilly wanted all of you to know. "Dad loved to hear me sing. I loved when Dad covered me with kisses. He was the first to see me when I was born. My daddy caught me in his arms and was proud to deliver me." So I will say, Andrea, you bore her and Chris caught her. And that's the way that it should have been, I believe.

Not only was he a family man, he was a man's man. He was an outdoorsman. He loved, as we said, being outside in God's creation, hunting, having fun. I am gonna say that his motor was always running all the time. And the word out in the country was one time they had this old Sea-Doo and it didn't run exactly right, so Chris put it in the pond and cranked it up and tried to run it. Now can you visualize that scene?

He, speaking of outdoors, was one of the driving forces at Cross Point with some of his closest friends with our Wild Game Dinner, which has become an annual event. We have a toy and coat giveaway that's a missional event for the sole purpose to serve the needy and hungry and poor children and those who are cold during the winter, which is close to the heart of God, according to Matthew 25.

Our giveaway day is on the first Saturday morning in December, and when we initially started doing that at Cross Point, we didn't anticipate the fact that people in this town would start camping out the night before on Friday and camp out all night in the bitter cold. And the first year they did that, Chris and some of these guys here just sprang into action. They didn't have to call me or the leadership at Cross Point. They just sprang into action. They brought heaters and they brought food and they brought blankets and hand warmers and they spent the night with those people who were waiting to get in in the morning to be fed and given toys for their children to have for Christmas and a coat to wear.

So many started trying to make provisions each year to do that better, not being able to stand the fact that nobody ought to have to stand outside for food or clothes in the cold weather. And so, this group kept bringing us their suggestions, one of which was from Chris. And it was to put on a wild game event in August, so you could eat anything that you could stomach and there would be items, auction items that you could bid on and have and take home, and it was all for one reason—every dollar was gonna be given to be given away. To the church to be given away. And we've done it for two years and we bring in a speaker and he speaks a thought from the word of God and it's a fun evening.

Last year, and Chris was the one beating the bushes in this town, asking people to donate and come to it, last year they gave the church for the giveaway, cause it's not a budgeted thing, they gave the church $14,000 to go serve the poor and needy children. It was $14,000, in two years it's almost $25,000.

And so one of the challenges I want to issue to you is this: There's one way you can honor his life, is to go and do something unselfish and kind to bless someone, a child, the needy, the hungry, the poor, and the cold. Do it in the name of Jesus. Do it to keep Chris' memory and life alive. And if you want to help his buddies here to carry that light and legacy on, then come support our Wild Game Dinner in August. Or call out and see how you can help. Or come serve about five hundred needy families on that first Saturday in December, and you'll be blessed.

How do you measure a man? It's whether or not he's a family man, whether or not he had a heart for God and a heart for people and a servant's heart, and thirdly you measure a man by the friends he has and keeps. The Bible says he that has friends must show himself friendly, and you could put his picture right there beside that verse.

Jeremiah told his people that because they had

gotten a long way away from God and weren't serving Him and their city, that things were gonna happen to them and they would go to Babylon and they would happen, but once they got there God then told him to tell his people to go work for the peace and prosperity of the city. And so I too want to commend all of you who work for the peace and the prosperity of the city. And for every lighthouse and congregation of God's people that's working for the peace and prosperity of the city. And I want to tell all of you guys, that if you ever need anything particularly of the spiritual nature, we'll be there. Because you got a friend. And the same is true to your family as well.

Keep pressing on. He was a man of great friend and conviction. And I'm proud to say that not only were we brothers in Christ but we were friends. And so I want to say two things as we close. Last Wednesday night, he and Andrea sat behind Summer and I at our Peak of the Week Bible class. They were there mid-week services because they wanted to be. And intellectually we know how fast things can happen and how quickly they can turn, but we never think it's gonna happen to us tonight. So he walked into our outreach center, and he asked two of his buddies, "You wanna go frog giggin' Friday night?" It's another reason why today's so tough. But I'm going to say, even though we didn't have time to prepare, when you live prepared and ready, you don't have to get ready. And that's a great lesson for us.

And so, as you guys sat behind us and we sang, I wanna share with you for everyone here, some of the words, the truths that Chris sang Wednesday night. And by the way, I know all of you believe I'm telling the truth, but he sang unusually loud that night, didn't he? And so, would you just listen to some of the truths that he proclaimed: "Light of the world, you stepped down into darkness, opened my eyes and let me see. Beauty that made this heart adore you, hope of a life spent with you. So here I am to worship. We are a moment, you are forever. Lord of the ages, God before time. We are a vapor, you are eternal. Let the glory of your name be the passion of the church. Let the song of Christ be the measure of our lives. Don't you wanna go to that land? Don't you wanna go to that land? There's nothing but peace in that land. I need you more, more than yesterday. I need you more, more than words can say. My hope is built is nothing less than Jesus' blood and righteousness. And I dare not trust the sweetest frame, but wholly lean on Jesus' name. When darkness comes to hide his face, I rest on His unchanging grace. In every high and stormy gale, my anchor holds within the veil."

And so Andrea told me something Saturday that I'll never forget. With faith and courage that only God can provide, and with a rock solid conviction, "I'm going to tell the evil one that he will not destroy us. He didn't when Travis passed." He didn't when many of you have been in these same shoes, and he will not defeat us now.

So in the words of Romans 8, that I shared with his church family yesterday, I'm going to close by sharing with you today. I consider that our present sufferings are not worth comparing with the glory that will be revealed in us. For we know that the whole creation's been groaning, as in the pains of childbirth right up to this present time, but what shall we say in response to all of this? If God be for us, who can be against us? He who did not spare His own Son but gave Him up for us all. He will graciously give us all things. In all things we are more than conquerors through Him who loved us. For I am sure than neither death nor life, nor angels nor rulers, nor things present nor things to come, not powers, not height nor depth, nor anything else in all creation, will be able to separate us from the love of God in Christ Jesus our Lord. And if you agree with that would you say "I do."

I too want to tell you what we're gonna do. We are gonna leave here praising God for Chris Williamson. And we are going to, as Ronnie asked us to do, pray and pray and pray like we've never prayed before for this family. For every one of you. And we're going to go out of here being kinder to each other. And we're going to go out of here looking for a needy person to serve. And we're going to look up and look around and see who we can serve and we're gonna look within and so to all of you, may God bless and keep you, may the Lord make His face shine upon you and be gracious to you, may He turn His face towards you and give you all His everlasting peace.

Would you bow with me please?

Dear father, we praise You for the life of Chris Williamson and the legacy of the lives that live on. The fact that he was a servant, it still speaks to us and we are grateful that he was a child of Yours, a brother in Christ, a friend. We claim the power of the resurrection today, and we thank You that sin, death, and Satan has not and will not conquer and defeat us. We thank You that nothing can separate us from Your love. So help us to hold on to Your unchanging hand. Help us to hold onto this precious family and surround them with our prayers and with our love and with our deeds. And help us all to live as Chris did, to live ready, and not miss the joy. And dear Father we can only imagine what You have in store for all of us who love You and follow You and long for Your appearing. We ask You to accept everything that's been said and done for Your honor and glory, and help us live for You and for others. It's in the name of Your Son, and Chris' Savior, and our Savior that we pray, Amen.

"See You Again" played next. And then "The Dance."

Afterwards, the pallbearers (his co-workers along with the eight who would be carrying him) exited the building, and the respectful men from the funeral home began wheeling the casket up the long aisle of the church, with our family following behind. I walked behind my husband for the last time. My best friend in the world. The one I so desperately needed now more than ever. The one person I needed to have his arms around me saying, "It's ok, Andrea, I'm here." My Earthly strength. My biggest support. I was so overwhelmed with trying to process and comprehend the reality of this moment. There were many times we had walked that aisle at Jackson Heights visiting church services there with Gary, Tammra, Heather and Billy. We had sung songs of praise there together, prayed and listened to God's word many times— together. And now, it was just all different. Emptiness consumed me. And as we walked behind that wooden casket holding my dearest friend and our family's rock, reality of it hit Lilly in ways I can only imagine her six-year-old mind could process. She began to weep, and I did the only thing I knew to do. I picked her up and carried her the rest of the way. What else would a parent do but console and carry a broken-hearted child? It's exactly what the good Lord was doing for me.

As we left the church following a hearse carrying our family's provider, protector and comforting husband and father, the kids and I had no idea what we would witness on our route to the cemetery. Chris' brother Billy was allowed to drive his service truck in front of the hearse as an escort, which was a tremendous honor. As we were driven by my dad, we came upon a church parking lot on the way, which was filled with Florence Electricity Department trucks—service trucks, pick-up trucks, bucket trucks and others with their buckets and lifts raised to the sky as a salute to Chris. His co-workers/friends/brothers lined the road, standing in front of the trucks, with their hands, caps and hard hats held to their hearts. I have never seen anything more beautiful in my life. What an honor! What an amazing tribute to their fallen brother! So much respect. I remember my dad and me telling the kids to be sure and really look and take all of that in. It was amazing. It was honorable. It was so incredibly special. It was memorable. And breathtaking. Just like Chris. I wanted that vision imprinted on their minds, and mine, forever.

As we approached the cemetery, two trucks with their buckets lifted to meet at the top formed an archway for us to drive under to lay Chris to his final resting place. There were policemen there also who were not required to be, but who wanted to show respect for another city servant. Witnessing those beautiful visions of honor caused me to experience, for the first time, my heart breaking from pain and beaming with pride all at the same time. Fortunately for me, I have been able to experience that many times since. Chris has been honored and remembered in such beautiful ways; my heart has learned to accept and embrace several different emotions coming out all at once. I like to call it multi-tasking of the heart. It is an amazing thing.

As we parked at the cemetery and tried to prepare our minds and spirits for what we had to experience now, I turned to my dad. "Did you talk to the director to be sure he understands what I want?" We had had a conversation on the way to the church that morning, and I told him I wanted to do for Chris what we had done for my brother Travis. I wanted us to be the first to shovel scoops of dirt onto his casket. After me and any family and friends that wanted to take part, I wanted Chris' co-workers to be able to if they wanted. I didn't want anyone to be stopped. I didn't want us to be rushed. My dad assured me that the director understood and that what I wanted would be carried out as requested.

As we went to sit down graveside for the last service, Brody said he couldn't come up there with us. He said he did not want to shovel dirt. So, my mom stayed back away from the crowd with him. Again, I let the kids make some decisions of what their young souls could bear. I knew the entire experience was traumatic enough.

After our minister said the final prayer and Chris' casket was lowered into the ground, my girls and I walked up, and after me, they each shoveled a scoop onto their daddy. I wanted to see this thing through to the very end. I didn't want a stranger covering him. I wanted him literally covered by love. After family and some friends participated, Brody eventually decided he could come and take part. I was so thankful he did. There were friends of Averee and Brody who also helped.

Then Chris' co-workers, all wearing their work uniforms, stood in line to honor their brother and friend. I remember watching those strong, masculine men, some almost sobbing at first, coming up one at a time, and the pain you saw in them as they shoveled. After the first man went, he went to the back of the line. They didn't stop. They were like me and wanted to see this out to the end for Chris. They didn't want to quit him. And they didn't. Not until the last speck of dirt leveled the ground. There was an obvious healing taking place in them. I remember each time one of them would come up, it looked easier emotionally. It was cleansing their souls, and mine. I felt such a comfort knowing I had asked them to help me do something that was also helping them. As weird as it sounds to say, seeing as how they were covering my husband's body with dirt, it was beautiful. Crazy to say, I know. But I've learned that excruciating experiences are beautiful also. The deepest pain can be beautiful.

During the midst of the Florence Electricity Department guys respecting Chris with that act of love, Chris' mom and I were experiencing a somewhat amusing moment together. A tiny green grasshopper had jumped on Kay while we sat next to one another. First it got on her shoulder and stayed for a few minutes, then on top of her head, then onto me, then back to Kay. It went on for several minutes, and gave us a smile and some relief from the pain. We chose to believe it was a sign—of Chris being ok and hope for what was to come. Truth is, the remainder of the summer was filled with visits to me and the kids and Kay from many little green grasshoppers. Believe what you will, but it hasn't happened any other summer. You just have to look for and acknowledge those God signs. They're definitely there.

After the last speck of ground was covering Chris' body and flowers were placed on top, we walked away from his Earthly resting place. I knew without any doubts that I had exhausted everything I could to honor this precious man who had blessed the Earth for thirty-nine short, but full-of-life years. I was thankful to the Father for holding us up through the most exhausting days of our lives. I was comforted by all the love and respect that had been shown to our family through those first several days. I was relieved that for a moment, no important decisions needed to be made. And I was still so scared to face this new world without him. I was nervous to take on these new roles as widow and single mom, without my best friend. Yet I did what I knew was needed at that moment. The only decision I had to make at the time: I got in the car with the kids, took a deep breath, and my dad drove us home.

He later reminded me of a conversation I had forgotten from that day on June 9, 2014. After we pulled up at home from the cemetery and the kids got out, we kept sitting there. I asked him, "Daddy, what do I do now?" He said that one day I would wake up and I would decide to live and choose to be happy again. This came from the man who had lost his son and literally had to learn to live and be happy again. I saw him and my mom do it. I knew it was possible, despite the overwhelming pain and anxiety and fear. They were my biggest proof. One hundred percent. If they could withstand the storm of losing their boy and hold onto their faith, and find joy and peace and happiness again, I knew without a shadow of a doubt I could and would do the same.

It was time to go into our home and try to live a new life, a completely new and scary life.

"May the God of hope fill you with all joy and peace in believing, so that by the power of the Holy Spirit you may abound in hope."

–Romans 15:13

"For I consider that the sufferings of this present time are not worth comparing with the glory that is to be revealed to us."

–Romans 8:18

"And after you have suffered a little while, the God of all grace, who has called you to His eternal glory in Christ, will himself restore, confirm, strengthen, and establish you."

–1 Peter 5:10

"The Lord is my light and my salvation; whom shall I fear? The Lord is the stronghold of my life; of whom shall I be afraid?"

–Psalm 27:1

Chapter 6

THE FIRST YEAR

I'm thankful it was summer when Chris passed, while the kids were out of school. We didn't need the stress of homework and tests and other activities. We didn't need a bedtime or a schedule. We simply needed time — time to mourn, to cry, or just to lie down and rest when the exhaustion overtook us. We also needed time to play and swim and go out in the yard and feel the sun and warmth and let God's voice tell us He was still there. The Lord blessed us with that time to be able to just recover some and try and adjust to the new, challenging reality of our new life without Chris.

I wasn't sleeping well for the first time in my life. I was always such an easy sleeper, roll over and I was out. Until now. I would lie in bed for hours until maybe 1:00 or 1:30 in the morning, wake up a few more times, and be up by 5:30 or 6. Mornings were the toughest for me. That's one of the reasons I included the word *rise* in the title of this book. I had to rise every morning with faith that God would get me through it. I would wake up, and it would take me five or ten seconds before reality would set in again. *Chris is gone. He is really gone. Still. Today is the same as yesterday. I wasn't dreaming. This is my life now.* So I would cry and then get determined and get up. I was usually very nervous and didn't want to be on medication if I could function without it, so I took several natural supplements to help calm me. Thankfully they helped. I found solitude in spending time on our back porch every morning, listening to God's creatures and using this quiet time to pray and get myself together before the kids got up. I would go through this routine in the morning, and through the day things would get easier and my mind would adjust to the knowledge of Chris' absence. Then bedtime would come, and the process would repeat.

Some people have been surprised that nighttime wasn't as difficult for me as the morning. It was definitely a challenge for me but not as much as the reality check I would endure every a.m. See every morning between six and six-fifteen (and sometimes six-twenty-five, which was fun) Chris and I would get up for the day. Ninety percent of the time I would pack him a lunch while he got a shower and dressed for work. Someone told me before I got married that whatever I did that first year, he would expect from then on. Wanting to be a good little wife and help my hard-working husband, I started packing his lunch on workdays as soon as we came home from our honeymoon. And oh there were so many times I wished I hadn't gotten him used to it, especially once all three kids were in school and it meant me packing four lunches every morning. However, no matter the complaints in my head, I took pride in that small task every day. He appreciated it, and I liked taking care of him.

So every morning after Chris went to Heaven, I desperately missed that morning routine. I missed the lunch packing (and sometimes breakfast too when we actually got up on time), and the hug and kiss goodbye, the "be careful" as he rushed out the door, watching his truck pull out of the driveway, and appreciating the hard-working job he was headed to. It took me quite a long time for mornings to be easier and for me to be able to wake up without having to remind myself of his absence.

I remember getting his lunchbox back. I took the dishes out but left that ice pack and napkin in there for I can't even remember how long. And the lunchbox stayed on the kitchen counter in its spot for months after his passing. Obviously I knew it wouldn't be used again, but I just couldn't let it go. I wasn't ready to accept the knowledge of never packing it again. And then finally one day I looked at it, and my heart was strong enough to put it away. That's what is amazing about grief. You do what you can when you are ready. And no one can tell you when that is.

After a few weeks the kids and I settled back into somewhat of a summer schedule. We returned to church (after two weeks because Father's Day hit the following Sunday and that was definitely not a good idea), summer softball scrimmages for Averee continued, and we began getting out more with friends for the typical out-of-school activities: movies, bowling, swimming and lunch dates.

I had the shifts at our boutique covered most of the time, mainly because I wanted to be with the kids as much as possible before school started back and because my nerves weren't ready for dealing with a lot of customers. I was very blessed to have responsible young women to help me out and take care of things there.

It was good to be somewhat busy again, to help distract our minds from constantly feeling the void at our house. Being home was safe, safe from the craziness of the outside world which took my nerves to levels I had never experienced, safe from almost screaming in public or wanting to have a complete meltdown in a crowd of people, safe from having to look up at power lines while sitting at a red light or meeting a Florence Electricity Department truck on the road and having to hold myself back from thinking, *Is that Chris?*

At home I didn't have to fear the uncomfortable situations of running into friends and acquaintances. You've been there, on one side or the other. People can't win. If they ask you the awkward question of "How are you?", then you may give them the *how do you think I am?!* look, and if they don't mention anything about it, then they might appear to not care. So it's somewhat of a lose-lose. I always felt sorry for them. I wanted to start the conversation myself and say, "Please don't be weird around me. I won't break into a million pieces. I will hold my emotions back as hard as I can so you don't feel more uncomfortable. I know you just care. And you feel bad for me, and that's ok. But even though I am changed forever, I'm still Andrea. Just a different Andrea. And it hurts, but it's ok. Please pray for me and my children, and that's more important than anything else you could ever do. Please don't ever tell me all you know to do is pray. I am honored by your prayers. Thank you for loving us. I see it in your eyes. I know your heart. Even if you can't find the right words, it's ok. I know." If I could have just done that! I was just too emotionally unstable. I would have broken down by the fourth or fifth word. I had to keep the public conversations as casual and brief as possible. Over time, and several months, these run-ins became easier (at least for me), and I didn't fear the grocery store and other public areas as much.

Not only was home the safe place; it was also incredibly sad. I yearned to be there when I wasn't, but at home Chris' absence was undeniable. We couldn't avoid it. He was constantly not there. He was constantly not pulling in the driveway, not sitting at the table with us to eat, not dirtying clothes or leaving a dirt trail on the floor from his work boots. Seriously, I could have never imagined how much I would miss that extra laundry, dirty dishes, and even sleeping pants lying in the corner of our bedroom floor. I missed hearing the shower in the morning while I was in the kitchen. I missed the chit-chat we had and me handing him his lunch and kissing him goodbye. The texts and calls. I missed knowing he was working so hard for us every day, never complaining. I missed hearing him say "helloooooo" in such a happy voice as he walked in the door every afternoon around 3:50. I missed the warm fuzzy feeling of cooking a nice meal for our family and feeling like I was rewarding my husband for being such a hard worker and provider. I missed the prayers and laughs and important decisions we shared around our kitchen table. Now we had the empty seat with a spotlight on it reminding us he wasn't there. I quickly began sitting in Chris' chair at the table. It was the best way to keep me from being able to look at the emptiness.

I missed seeing him throw ball in the afternoons with Brody or seeing the two of them sit in the chair every night watching television. I missed hearing him sing with Lilly or listening to her squeals and his laughter as he stole her kisses. I missed seeing him coach Averee on softball in the front yard and witnessing the pride on his face at one of her musical performances. He wasn't there with me every night helping me get the kids to bed. No one to talk to in bed, to discuss our dreams and future. To hold me. To comfort me. No Chris. Nowhere at our house. And then maybe strangely for some, he was everywhere. I felt him all around us. That gave me comfort. I felt like God was giving me that gift to know that he wasn't far. There were moments of quietness and completely being aware that I closed my eyes and I would have sworn he was all around me. It was such a gift. Despite him physically not being there, feeling him kept me from going completely insane.

I had a few experiences early on that some might would say were delusional, but I believe in the depths of my soul were sent straight from Heaven. A few mornings the week after, I woke up to a sound that is still indescribable with words. I can only use the word majestic to come close to a description — A combination of a harp and chimes perhaps. All I know is it woke me up in the most peaceful, calm way, and as soon as the sound ended I yearned to hear it again. Was it God allowing me to experience a little taste of Chris' new world? I like to think so. I know this: I've never heard anything so beautiful before.

Another experience I had that was only a few days after his accident, when I was in bed one night and was desperately asking Chris to do something, anything to let me know he was still close. I honestly would have been ok with a lamp flying across the room at that time if only he could have made it happen. That didn't occur, but I closed my eyes and I opened my heart completely and asked God to just let Chris reach me in some way. As I type these words knowing some won't believe, I still feel the need to share. As I lay in bed with my eyes closed but my mind and spirit completely opened, I saw Chris' face and heard these words: "I'm ok, Andrea. I'm ok. I'm ok. I am ok." I could see him right in my face and hear him with every "I'm ok" saying the words over and over to convince me and reassure me. The way I heard the words is exactly how Chris would have said them. He would have been drilling it into my mind over and over to give me comfort and peace. Believe it as reality or my imagination, but either way, it worked. I was thankful to God for it. And I knew it. He was ok. He had been ok. Now I had to convince myself that I would be ok.

No matter how much faith you possess, nothing prepares you for the "after" of such a tragic loss. You don't even know where to begin. For me, my entire life is divided by this monumental event. The before and the after. There are sentences often with "before Chris passed" or "since Chris passed." This is true for any loss because it changes everything in our lives. Nothing is the same, ever. Our reality has shifted. It's like we went to bed one night and began this crazy dream that never ends. Or that we went to bed and woke up on a different planet where everything is the same, except this extremely important part of our life is gone. It really is starting over, living in a new world as I like to say. It feels like you are in slow motion and the world keeps spinning and you just want the world to slow down with you. But it keeps on going like before, like nothing has happened.

When someone is such a huge piece of our lives, and suddenly our puzzle isn't complete anymore, it's so difficult to get our minds adjusted to the fact that we have to create a new puzzle, one without this piece. It's as if someone took this perfect masterpiece and shattered it and we are expected to create it again—but in a different form with a new set of eyes. It seems impossible. Thankfully with God all things are possible and that belief is what we must grasp and use to rebuild our new life. It brings new challenges and a completely different perspective, a perspective that you wish everyone had, without having to experience the Earth-shattering pain that delivers it to you, a perspective that helps you appreciate every moment more, that keeps you from complaining as much, one that is the key to surviving the pain, to seeing the good in every aspect. I learned early to search every day for the good, to fight for every ounce of it, to let it motivate me to keep going.

Our first holiday: July fourth. We didn't know what to expect with holidays after Chris' accident, except to miss him even more. You know what happens to those extra special days of spending time with your favorite people? They become the most dreaded. The happiness is overshadowed by the emptiness. The crowds only remind you of your loneliness. You strive for laughter and happiness, and though you may find it, the pain is just as prevalent.

Our first holiday was spent with family, striving for some fun and joy, knowing it was still a better option than just being home. We spent the day at Kay's with Chris' family, swimming and enjoying chicken stew and homemade ice cream and just doing our best at being happy or at least getting through it. Honestly I spent part of the time in the house searching for a quiet place to calm my nerves. But the kids had fun with cousins and we did what we needed to do. The night was spent at my parents with more family, and we watched fireworks that night like normal and ended the day with peace and relief.

The next day brought about another huge first for us. One month. I'm not exactly sure what it is about the date. Once a tragic event takes place, that date becomes a reoccurring anniversary, every month. At least for me it was. In the beginning, I hated Thursdays. Every one that rolled around was dreaded, and I counted the weeks for the longest. But the fifth, it felt like a knife. I didn't know how I would feel about it—and didn't really think about how I would feel about it—until it was upon us for the first time that July. It seems with every milestone (week, month, etc.), more certainty of the new reality is revealed. The fog is lessened perhaps. It makes it seem more set in stone. Even though you know they are gone and it is permanent, your mind and heart still want them back so much that maybe you keep yourself somewhat protected in the realm of disbelief. And then these dates, they pull you out of that bubble and seem to scream at you to wake up from the dream of hope. That is the only way I know to explain why they are dreaded so much. We spent our day of that one month anniversary where I knew we needed to, visiting with Chris' parents.

Thankfully the first week of August brought us some excitement. I had planned for over a month a trip to St. Louis with the kids and my mom to visit my uncle and aunt and cousin there and to watch the Red Sox play the Cardinals. Chris had become a Red Sox fan several years before, and he and Brody loved watching the games together. Not long before Chris passed away, I remembered him telling me they would be in St. Louis that summer, and it was so much closer to home than Boston. I always loved visiting our family there growing up, and I knew the kids would love it too. What made it even better is that we know Josh Willingham, who had just retired from the MLB, and he made a few calls and got us on-field passes for warm up, and they were going to do everything possible to get Dustin Pedroia (Chris and Brody's favorite player) to come talk to Brody before the game. We. Were. Ecstatic.

We enjoyed our time in St. Louis, and the night of the game was incredible. Kay and Maw ended up getting tickets and coming, and Chris' uncle Will and his family came too. Brody and Averee and I got our passes and stood on that field for a few hours, watching both teams warm up. And sure enough, Dustin Pedroia came out and visited for a few minutes, took pictures with both of the kids, and signed a few things for them. He was the nicest guy, and it seemed like such a magical night, even though the Sox lost. Having such a special night helped me cope with this fifth of the month, which marked two months. All I could picture was Chris' big smile across his face. What a blessing!

By the second week of August we were back home, and the

kids were beginning a new school year. Averee started seventh grade, Brody the third, and Lilly the first. The first day of school hit on Brody's birthday, which was extremely difficult. Two important events without Chris. It was two firsts on the same day. Firsts are the worst. They really are. If you've ever experienced severe loss and grief, you know this. Maybe because with every first comes another reality check. It makes it more official that your loved one isn't coming back here. The days that are usually the most anticipated and exciting of the year become the most dreaded in so many ways.

I had decided to go back home and not work that day so I could take goodies to school for Brody's class and just deal with whatever emotions would come my way. So there I was, alone that morning at our house (which was usually bad anyway), and I was a wreck. The chaos of the kids being around kept me distracted from breaking down as much most days. And now I wouldn't have that five days a week. I was having withdrawals from the kids and dealing with the pain of not having Chris here for Brody's ninth birthday and the first day of school. It was a bad, bad day. I remember thinking, *Is this how I'm going to feel every birthday from now on? Every special day of the year? Is every exciting day of the year now going to be the most terrible day?* I held onto hope for good. I tried with all my might to refocus my energy and pray for the Lord to guide me through it. Eventually I got my mind back to a good place, one of appreciation and peace. *My kids were healthy, I was healthy and here with them, and most importantly it was a day of celebration of the birth of my son. How could I not find good in those truths? How could I not be grateful for what God had blessed us with?*

When it was time to pick the kids up, I put on a smile and was genuinely happy to have them with me and tell me all about their day. We went home and we visited and ate together and had cake together, and we all knew that we had achieved a great milestone that day. God got us through two big firsts in one day. What an accomplishment! It was just more proof that we could do this. With the challenges and pain of it, with God we could get through.

September 25, 2014. Chris' co-workers had invited me to come to work, as they were placing a plaque on a memorial stone that is there in memory of employees who have lost their lives while working at the department. I was very honored and agreed to be there as a few of them spoke words about Chris and what he meant to them, we prayed, and then one of them attached the plaque with his name on the stone alongside others who had previously passed. It almost seemed like another memorial service, and, well, I guess that's exactly what it was.

It has always been painful and comforting for me to be around those guys. There's difficulty in seeing them all in their work uniforms and with those trucks because it reminds me of the countless times I saw him wearing his uniform and driving his service truck home, relieving me of worry and fear. Each time I see one of them I am reminded of the many loads of laundry I washed, scrubbing out oil stains and mud and many times them already being wet because of the elements he would work out in. It reminds me of him walking up at the ballfield because he had hurried from work and didn't take time to change because he didn't want to miss a second of one of our kids playing ball.

When I see one of those huge bucket trucks, I'm reminded of the times I would unknowingly meet Chris on the road and he would immediately call me and say, "Well, I waved at you and you didn't even see me!" I would always say, "Well, I didn't know it was you! I don't want to be the weirdo that waves at every truck!" We always got a good laugh out of each other. Many times since I wish I had been that weirdo. But then I might have missed out on those laughs.

The day at the Florence Electricity Department when Chris was honored with that plaque, another memory is extremely valuable to me. One of his former co-workers, who had already retired but wanted to be there that day to honor Chris, shared something with me, reiterating what I knew of Chris' character. He told me, "You know when it's raining or in the afternoon when all the guys are in the crew room sitting around talking? Well, you know sometimes guys will talk about women or just things they shouldn't talk about. If Chris was ever sitting somewhere and someone started talking about something like that, he would always get up and move. He wouldn't say anything, but he never was a part of one of those conversations. I just thought you should know that." What a blessing for me to hear! I knew his heart, but hearing from a co-worker that Chris showed that example at work made me so proud.

It also made me proud to hear from many of his friends and co-workers that all he ever talked about was me and the kids and how proud he was of his family. And his God. He shared his faith with those guys. He didn't brag to me about that. I never knew it. But several of them said he would stay after work and talk to them about church and their spiritual lives. What a testament of his spiritual life! The sharing of those witnesses of his other family, the ones he spent the other half of his days with, encouraged me to be a light like Chris was, to be that example, that living example.

Those first few months of the fall were spent at volleyball and basketball courts and dance classes and various school activities. The kids were doing the best they could, being at school in a classroom trying to concentrate all day, which I've said many times I couldn't have done. My nerves were too bad to sit still and quiet and try and concentrate. I am so proud of the three of them for not complaining and for being so strong. There were some issues with Brody — not misbehaving or making bad grades, but with being able to focus in class — brought to my attention. Thankfully I had a counselor from The Healing Place (a grief clinic we had been visiting) reassure me. Brody didn't have attention issues. He was just a child experiencing grief. I received support from his teacher and principal that we would work together to keep him as focused as possible despite the pain that was sometimes overwhelming his mind in class. The girls also had times that were very difficult, and the counselors at school helped us with that as well.

October was still busy with school and ball and thankfully with a few vacations. The second week of the month we went on a beach trip with Kay and Maw and Chris' sister Noel and her son

Issac. I dreaded going back to the beach for the first time without Chris, but we had a great time—lots of wave jumping and sand digging and seafood eating and fun. We shared lots of laughs, and it was just an overall enjoyable trip.

Halloween weekend we went back on our Gatlinburg trip with the Williamsons, and it was also a memorable one. We were surprised to wake up the first morning in the mountains to lots of snow, which was unusual for Gatlinburg in October, and that brought about some fun memories. We had a good time and reminisced a lot about the previous one and all the fun Chris had.

The biggest holidays of the season rolled around fairly quickly, and I have to admit I was terrified of them. First came Thanksgiving. Surprisingly, when the week was upon us, I felt calm and peaceful about it. I asked for prayers from close friends, and I lifted us up more with the hope that the thankfulness would outweigh the sadness. And for the most part it did. We spent the day with family and lots of food and found comfort in that time together.

At the same time came the painful decision to sell Chris' herd of cattle. I had been talking about it for a few months, as I knew it was inevitable. Cows had been such an important part of his life. His granddaddy, Paw, had cows, and Chris had inherited that love from him. Paw let him have cows on his land with his, and when Paw passed away, Chris' grandmother sold Paw's to Chris and allowed him to keep the herd on her land next to us. So they were always there, right next door, for us to see and hear and help feed. One of the cows, who we named Essie, was given to Chris by

Paw when I was pregnant with Averee. She wouldn't nurse, so we bottle fed her, and she became a pet to us. She would let Chris put Averee on her back and still to this day will come up to you and let you pet her.

The day after Chris' accident, Kay came over to the house after being at Maw's. She said, "Andrea, I have been lying in momma's bed and those cows won't stop bawling. They have been bawling all day." I had not heard them because our house was full of people and noise, and I wasn't close enough to the pasture. But I noticed the next few days that any time I was outside, they were indeed bawling. They didn't have any needs and had not been getting fed anything other than pasture grass. Chris didn't go out there every day. But they knew something was wrong. The world was different. It was like when you take a calf off to the sale barn and the momma cries for a few days. It was strange and incredible at the same time. Folks, there's obviously so much more than our human eyes can possibly see.

I knew when it was starting to turn cold and they would have to be cared for more with feed and hay, I would have to let them go. What a painful release. The kids and I had a difficult time with the decision even though I knew it needed to be made. I just couldn't sell Essie. Chris had always said she would die out there because he would never be able to sell her. My dad said I could put her on his pasture, and to this day she's still a part of our family.

Thankfully, Chris' cousin's husband had an uncle who had cattle—and wanted to buy the herd. It kept us from having to sell them to strangers and made the transition a little easier. We went to the pasture that day and looked at them awhile, shed some tears, and let go of another important part of our lives. Another big change. And it hurt, terribly, but we got through it.

December brought about dread and adjustments, as I for the first time didn't have Chris to help me decide on gifts and shop for the kids and come up with fun surprises. It was the first year since 1999 that I wouldn't shop for him. I had to keep reminding myself that he didn't need gifts. Not physical ones anyway. I realized Christmas would be the toughest holiday, and I remember feeling like I was literally preparing for battle. I was determined to fight all the bad feelings and sadness with my focus on good and wanting our kids to have an incredible Christmas despite the challenge of it. The only gift that I could give Chris was finding every ounce of happiness that I could, grabbing hold of it, passing that on to our children, and remembering him through it. That's what I decided to do: honor his memory, remember him, and help our family cope. I could handle that. And if I couldn't, I prayed the Lord would take over and handle it for me.

December 8, 2014. The president of the IBEW (International Brotherhood of Electrical Workers) local union 558 had asked me and the kids to come to the hall that night to hang a plaque on the wall in memory of Chris. We got there to see a room full of union members, including lots of Chris' co-workers. When it was time for me to go up to the front to hang it on the wall, one of the guys from the Florence Electricity Department came and walked me over to the center of the room at the back. All the guys there from the FED lined up on each side of the aisle for me to walk through. I could barely walk through the emotion. What an incredible honor! The respect they had for Chris was being passed on to me. And I couldn't respect them more than I did at that moment in time. They were determined to honor their friend and brother in every way possible, and I was more grateful than words could ever express. They gave me a gift that night of love and support and showing honor and respect to Chris.

My mom planned a trip for us a few days before Christmas to go to Nashville and spend the night at the Gaylord Opryland Hotel and do some fun holiday activities there. We decided a way we wanted to bless some strangers in Chris' memory, so the kids decorated a poster board before leaving that said, "Merry Christmas in memory of our dad Chris Williamson E-111," and they signed their names. They took turns holding the poster out the window of the car, and I paid for the order of the vehicle behind us in line. It thrilled the kids to see the faces of the people behind us when they realized what we had done. And it blessed my heart immensely to do it. We needed all the good feelings we could possible fill up with to help wash away the pain.

Christmas Eve that year came with a mixture of dread and excitement for the kids. We had been surprised every day that week with a surprise gift left anonymously at our house, which we found out later was from our church family staff members. That helped keep our spirits up. Also, I had asked for prayers from everyone I could think of and had people praying I had not even asked. Later Christmas Eve day, after we met my parents and brother and his family at the cemetery to remember my brother, we went to Wesley

Chapel cemetery to do the same for Chris. I remember telling the kids as we drove over, "You know I am really sad that your daddy is not here and I know this is gonna be tough, but I feel really peaceful. I can feel everyone's prayers, and I feel like God's arms are wrapped tightly around us holding us up." They all agreed that they felt the same way. I was so thankful.

I had put small Christmas trees in his vase holders, and Kay brought battery-operated candles to put at his headstone to glow during the night. Each of the kids placed a candle, we sang a few Christmas songs, and Brody read a scripture from the Bible. It was such a comforting act. Obviously it wasn't for Chris. He didn't need it. But we did. We needed that feeling in our heart of knowing we remembered him, that our love was just as strong, that although we were physically separated, the love we shared was incapable of being broken.

Christmas Eve night was spent with family, and although the void of Chris was undeniable, we had laughs and enjoyed our time together. Later it was time to go home and get ready for Santa.

Christmas morning, as dreaded and unusual for me as it was, was surprisingly joyful and filled with peace. I gave each of the kids something personalized and special to remember their daddy, and they enjoyed seeing their Santa surprises and just being kids. I know it had to be going through their minds, just like me. *He isn't here. I wish he was here. I need him to be here. It would be so much better with him here.* They were so strong. They let their excitement take hold and the spirit of Christmas come in and we had a good morning regardless.

The rest of Christmas day was as busy as usual, skipping from one house and get-together to another, lots of gift giving and receiving, and mountains upon mountains of food. God got us through the day in the happiest way possible. We shared memories of Christmases past when Chris was here and the fun times we shared. By the end of the day we were all exhausted, and I know for myself at least I felt like I had conquered the battle of Christmas. I felt a huge relief that fight was over.

We only had ten days until another big first was upon us–Lilly's seventh birthday. I was proud of us. Of course it had its difficulty, but I had been praying and praying and praying for strength and comfort and peace to get me through the week. See Lilly's birthday was on the third, and mine and Chris' wedding anniversary was the sixth. We would have been married fourteen years. That day hurt. I had by this time accepted the fact that I was now a single woman, although not at all by choice, and that first anniversary without Chris made the echo of my loneliness even louder.

I don't know what it's like to be divorced and having my marriage end in that way, but feeling like your marriage has been stolen and completely taken out of your hands is, well, it's the most helpless feeling. I never really knew what feeling alone meant, until I lost Chris. Even in a large crowd of people, I felt so alone. It was the strangest and hardest to describe feeling. I didn't know how to handle it, except cope with the uncomfortableness that consumed me and try to get through it. That January 6, 2015, the anniversary we couldn't celebrate, not by us choosing to end our marriage but by being separated without our will, it was a harsh reminder that my marriage was no more.

I had taken a step a few months earlier to try and accept the fact that as bad as I hated it, I was not married anymore. One day in November of 2014 I decided to take my wedding ring off. It wasn't planned. I was at my store and looking at my hand and just thought to myself, *maybe it's time*. I knew how much it was going to hurt, reminded by the nervousness that turned in my stomach. I honestly didn't know how I would handle it being off my finger, but it was one of those moments that the strength seemed to be there and the decision seemed to be made. So I took it off and spent the day staring at the red indention that was left from a ring I had worn for almost fourteen years. It was my moment of acceptance. I wasn't married anymore. I was a widow. As much as I hate that word, I tried with all my might to accept it. And I grieved that ring for several days. I feared that people would think I wanted to look single, which I didn't, and every bit of me wanted to put it back on and pretend for the rest of my life that I was still married. But I knew it was the best decision for me, and I struggled through the adjustment of my blank finger. Slowly, over the course of almost two years, that red indention on my left third finger faded and smoothed out, as it seemed to heal from the drastic change and void it experienced.

The next big holiday, unfortunately, was Valentine's Day. I've never cared much for the holiday. I feel like you should show the love of your life how much you admire them all year long, and participating in spending more money on superficial things doesn't prove true love, the kind that withstands marriage and kids and all challenges and messy things life is made up of. I always got Chris a gift, and he always did me too, usually flowers (which I always told him he didn't need to spend money on but always liked for him to spend money on); we just didn't make a big to-do about it all. But of course the holiday was painful. Walking in the grocery store to gigantic displays of balloons and candy and flowers and stuffed bears is never a good scenario when you don't have that person to buy the superficial stuff for. Again, I dealt with my uncomfortableness, the day passed, and I was surprised by several momma friends with gift cards for me and the kids to eat out on. Another comforting reminder of our blessings.

Spring came and was in full speed all around us, with softball starting up for Averee and baseball for Brody. It was bittersweet. All of it. The first softball season and baseball season without Chris. The seasons we were in right before he passed. Remembering all those last memories we had at those ball fields with him. I know it was hard on the kids, not having him there to cheer them on and help with their teams. They seemed to enjoy it as much as they could. So did I.

Averee's thirteenth birthday was April 19th, and again, I missed him immensely, as I know she did. She enjoyed the day with friends and we had a party welcoming the teen years, but of course with the thought in the back of my mind. *I'm now raising a teenager, alone.* It seems no matter how much energy goes into finding the good in every day and especially around holidays or special occasions, those thoughts will always be there. I believe it just echoes the love for that person. When I think that, I can't help but smile. The fact that I miss him that much proves how much I love him, and that makes me blessed, to have loved and still love a man that much. Wow. What a gift.

April 21, 2015. It was unplanned, but it was one of those tough decision days, and I finally went. After ten months and sixteen days, I found the strength on that day. I knew it would hit me at some point that it was time, and it did. Just out of nowhere that morning I thought, *It's a beautiful day and it's a good day to go.* I didn't want to, not at all, but I needed to. My soul needed it. I didn't tell anyone I was going except a few of Chris' friends from work that were there that night. I didn't even know where it was on Arlington Boulevard. I hadn't wanted to know. I still didn't that day, but sometimes you just know something difficult needs to be done and you suck it up and do it. I needed that accomplishment. I know that sounds weird to call it that, but trust me it was. It was what I had dreaded so much. *The place.* Where Chris' last moments on Earth took place. His last sights, thoughts, steps, conversations, smiles, laughs, phone calls, work. The place where he told me he loved me for the last time. I sat on that ground that April day, shed tears, and looked up at that pole and found some healing. I decided to look at that place as where Chris left here to redeem his Heavenly home. As much as it hurts to look at that pole and those lines, I know they aren't important. What's important is that Chris may be out of reach and far from here but not gone. Not gone at all. I was so thankful that Bill and Steve, friends and co-workers who happened to be there right after the accident, went with me. I'm forever grateful that they were there with him and prayed over him that night. Even though Chris physically didn't know they were there, I believe he knew. I can never put into my words my appreciation and respect for those guys who were there that night with Chris and experienced that traumatic and life-changing experience. They have always been in my prayers. And they always will be.

Four days after I defeated that mountain of dread and pain, it was the first birthday for me without him. I can't remember much, except that my mom and Kay made my two most favorite cakes in the world, and I told the kids I was going to spend the weekend eating them both. I pretty much kept that promise (haha). It was a difficult day for sure, but I was flooded with calls and messages and gifts from friends and family and was reminded of how very loved I am. It seems during the times I would have received gifts and extra love from Chris, I have always had special people step in and show me I am indeed still loved. My appreciation for that gift overflows.

After getting through April and quickly rolling right along into May, the reminiscing of the previous year became so much more frequent. We hit the eleventh month mark on the 5th, and then the dread snuck in at a swift pace that the one-year mark was more near than I wanted. May was a tough month anyway. So many last memories the year before with Chris. It was his last full month with us. It was his birthday month for crying out loud. Literally. If you are in the ocean of grief you know the two toughest days: their birthday and the day they went to Heaven. We were going to experience both within a two-week period. God had proven His strength in me, and I knew we would get through it, but I spent a lot of time in prayer and asked for God's grace and mercy to shower down on me constantly to get us through the best way possible. My number one goal was to protect the kids' spirits as much as possible.

I remember in 2014 on Chris' 39th birthday me telling him, "You know next year I'm going to be throwing you a shindig for the big 4-0!" We both laughed a little and that was all that was said. I never dreamed when I said it that we were celebrating his last one together, that he would never reach forty years on the Earth. As May 21st approached in 2015, the year he would have been the big 4-0, I talked to the kids about what they felt comfortable with and prayed about what I thought would be the most healing and easy-to-handle approach. I wanted to do something, but with us not ever experiencing this day before without him, I wanted to keep it as simple as possible. So, I talked with Kay and Gary and we decided for the immediate family to meet over at the cemetery that afternoon, sing happy birthday to Chris, release some birthday balloons, and eat cake in honor and memory of him.

Kay made what he always wanted her to make for his birthday, a mint chocolate brownie dessert, I brought "Over the Hill" plates and napkins, and we just all visited at the church pavilion and enjoyed the afternoon remembering and loving Chris. Yes, we had a little shindig after all. Again, not because he needed it but because we did. We needed to do something good that day and focus on still being able to celebrate him. It was still his birthday after all. Was it difficult? Absolutely. It always will be. But being able to keep on loving him and showing that love to him has healed us in multiple ways. I am so thankful I have led the kids in doing those things. My parents taught me that. And I have always tried to pass it on.

Not long after the birthday, we were finishing up school and getting ready to go back to the beach on our family vacation again with my parents, cousin, brother, and his family. It was going to be bittersweet—again, floods upon floods of memories from the year before. We went, had an amazing trip and held it together so well, made incredible memories, and came home to get ready for the summer.

There was still dread hanging over my head, as we approached June 5th. That anniversary day is hard. Actually the word *hard* doesn't begin to describe. Approaching that day, I wanted to do something at the pole on Arlington Blvd., and I decided to see if some of Chris' co-workers wanted to meet me there and hang some flowers on the pole. I didn't know if I could handle it on that day, so we went the night before, on June 4th. One of Chris' friends and work partners (Phillip) drove me, and the kids stayed home with Phillip's wife and kids. It was too difficult for them to go. To this day they still haven't gone to that place, and I will never pressure it. If they ever feel they can, I will take them. If not, no harm whatsoever.

Of course and without surprise, we pulled up to lines of trucks and cars and many amazing men and some wives who came for me, for themselves, and for Chris. I was scared even though I had been there before, even though I had walked the walk to that back yard before and had seen the spot. The pole. The lines. But still, as I approached that house and began the walk to the back, I could only think of the year before and of his last moments: Of him finding baby coons while he was working and trying to take care of them since their momma couldn't be found, of him walking up to the house next door and introducing himself to the young woman and telling her they would have them up and going soon, of him calling me at 7:26 p.m., right before he climbed back up the pole and it happened, of our last words to each other. "I love you." So many thoughts, and as I saw co-workers, some of whom had been there when it happened, my heart sank for them. I could only imagine what was replaying in their minds, and I prayed for them all.

I brought a card to attach to the flowers, all the guys there signed it, and after I hung them up, we all stood in a circle and prayed. I knew as difficult as it was, with every tear that was shed, we were healing more in that moment. I am convinced God laid it on my heart to go over there that night and to ask the ones that were forever changed by being his brother and friend and doing the same work to go with me. I know and understand it was too difficult for some to be there, and that's ok. But for the ones who did, I believe it was a massive step in recovering from the trauma of the event. If there's one thing I've learned, it's that sometimes the most difficult steps are the most healing and strengthen us in ways we don't always realize. I know for me, that night was exactly what I needed: another moment of honoring and remembering my husband.

June 5, 2015. One year. Coming back to the day it happened. His last day. I woke up early, as the guys at the electricity department had asked me to come up before their work day started and us have a few words and a prayer. Chris' dad met me there, and we all gathered at the memorial at work. A few men said some words, we all prayed, and of course we shared hugs and more tears. My dad has always said, letting those tears out leaves room for the good to come in. It was one of those times, one where I felt pain and peace reside in the same space at the same time.

My mom had come to stay with the kids that morning, and I was going to take home some breakfast. I drove over to Chick-fil-A, and as soon as I turned in, I hit something with my tire. I proceeded to the drive-thru and immediately noticed my tire was going flat quickly. I got out of line, parked my SUV, and called Gary to see if he could come help me. It was somewhat humorous to me. Of all days of the year, a flat tire on this day! He came and we got the spare on there, took it to get the tire repaired, and did have a little laugh about it. I told him I guess we needed more time together that day. Eventually my kids got their chicken biscuits.

That afternoon I was supposed to take them to the electricity department. Chris' co-workers wanted to plant a tree out at the memorial spot and thought it would be a good task for the kids. I loved the idea, something good to do, a new beginning. So we went and the guys gave each of the kids a hard hat and gloves to wear, and they each got to shovel dirt and water the Japanese maple tree and just hang out and visit with their daddy's friends. It was the best thing for them that day. And me. Absolutely perfect.

Our day ended at Kay's house. We went over to just hang out with her and spend the night and go to yard sales the next morning. She needed us, and we needed her. I knew we didn't need to be at home that night. We would be re-living things in our mind too much. So, we ate together and played ball together and got through that time of night staying busy and having fun with one another. It was just where we needed to be doing just what we needed to do.

Ending that day was a relief. I reflected a lot on the entire year, what we had experienced, and overcome. My mind constantly thought of the June 5th the year before, and how the events of that night had flipped our world upside down. I thought of how we had made it through the dreaded firsts, birthdays, anniversaries, holidays, ballgames, school programs, special events and the everyday moments that made up our life. Three hundred sixty-five days without him. Twelve fifths. Fifty-two Thursdays. It seemed like yesterday and forever all at the same time. My mind was overwhelmed when I thought of it. Along with the indescribable pain of it came pride, pride in how our God was bigger than the pain, how far He had carried us, how He had never left, appreciation that He had answered prayers, over and over and over again, every second of every minute of every hour and day of that year. The days that I prayed for Him to just hold me up and carry me through, He showed up and showed out every time. The times I had to just lie down because the exhaustion of grief was too much and I couldn't handle life at the time, He was there. When I watched

135

the kids doing anything and could barely swallow with the lump in my throat and my mind could only think *why isn't he here?*, my God wrapped His arms around me and was my biggest cheerleader and constantly told me I got through the most horrific day of my life and I could get through that one as well. He strengthened me. He comforted me. He sustained my weak and pitiful self. He told me I was enough. He told me I was His. He gave me peace when I thought it couldn't be found. He showed me joy when it seemed impossible. He shined light on me when the darkness seemed to overcome. He restored my soul over and over again, every day. When I called out to Him, He answered. When I gave it all over to Him, He used it for a good purpose. When I questioned His perfect plan and hated it at times, He said "Be still." And every second of every minute of every hour of every day, when all I knew to do was focus on that hour or minute or second and just get through it, He said, "Well done, my child." See in the darkest of times, in the waves of grief that sometimes cover you up and you feel as though another breath can't come, it is then that He is the most prevalent. It is then that you will feel Him the most. Whether the pain pushes you closer to Him or He pulls you into His arms when you don't have the strength, in those moments of weakness I believe it's the closest to God you can be.

I know for myself, I have never felt closer to God than I did during that year. Yes, I still feel close to Him, but when you are in such deep waters, you rely on Him much more. I have been taught a lesson in that I should constantly rely on Him and ask Him for that closeness. When all is great in your world, maybe you feel like you don't need your Father as much? I was guilty of that before. And even now at times. But I'm striving every day to keep that closeness, to keep relying just as much. He knows I need it. It's a tough lesson, one I was taught through the most magnitude of grief I have ever experienced.

The goal for me is to learn from these lessons. To me that is my purpose in this life: Live for Him and learn from Him. To take these lessons and be better. For myself. For my kids. To hopefully give hope to others in horrific pain. If not, what was the pain for? If I don't strive to improve myself and my soul, wow, what a waste it would be. We are all here for a purpose. Sometimes pain is a large part of it. The real test is whether we rely on God enough to take that pain and those experiences and still have enough faith and still have enough trust and enough hope in tomorrow and God's plan to ask him to hold us up through it until we can stand alone and give our testimony of His love. If I take these lessons and do that in my own life after the good Lord has gotten me this far, then my life is enriched and the good can cover up the bad and blow the smoke out of its flame. And that, my friends, is where happiness after tragedy can be found.

"The Lord is near to the brokenhearted and saves the crushed in spirit."

–Psalm 34:18

"He heals the brokenhearted and binds up their wounds."

–Psalm 147:3

"Trust in the Lord forever, for the Lord God is an everlasting rock."

–Isaiah 26:4

"The Lord is a stronghold for the oppressed, a stronghold in times of trouble. And those who know Your name put their trust in You, for You, O Lord, have not forsaken those who seek You."

–Psalm 9:10

"but they who wait for the Lord shall renew their strength; they shall mount up with wings like eagles; they shall run and not be weary; they shall walk and not faint."

–Isaiah 40:31

"And we know that for those who love God all things work together for good, for those who are called according to His purpose."

–Romans 8:28

Chapter 7
LESSONS

I would never be able to fit into one book all the lessons I have learned through loss and grief. God has taught me so much about my purpose in this life and about how to place my priorities and focus. I have learned these lessons because instead of only fixing my eyes on the pain and difficulty, I have searched for good and light and have opened myself up emotionally and mentally and spiritually asking the Lord to lead, guide and direct me to where I need to be. It is an everyday journey, one that is constantly changing as I learn more about myself and His plan for my life. I fail constantly. But I don't give up. Instead I constantly refocus and continue to grow through trust and reliance on Him and I am in constant awareness of His grace and mercy on my completely un-perfect self. I do want to share some of the most life-changing lessons and revelations that have come from the losses and grief I've experienced in my life.

The first, and I believe most important, lesson I have experienced through this is how faith seems to be the backbone of positive healing and the steering wheel leading you down the path to comfort and strength and peace. The right amount of faith needs to exist for the other answers to be revealed — the believing in what you cannot see, but still trusting and walking sometimes blindly, being guided by Him and those beliefs.

> *"Since we have the same spirit of faith according to what has been written, 'I believed, and so I spoke,' we also believe, and so we also speak, knowing that He who raised the Lord Jesus will raise us also with Jesus and bring us with you into His presence. For it is all for your sake, so that as grace extends to more and more people it may increase thanksgiving, to the glory of God. So we do not lose heart. Though our outer self is wasting away, our inner self is being renewed day by day. For this light momentary affliction is preparing for us an eternal weight of glory beyond all comparison, as we look not to the things that are seen but to the things that are unseen. For the things that are seen are transient, but the things that are unseen are eternal."*

–2 Corinthians 4:13-18

My favorite story of faith in the Bible is of Abraham in Genesis. I just can't imagine how distraught Abraham's spirit must have been when God commanded him to sacrifice Isaac. After Sarah being barren and God giving them the son He had promised (Genesis 21:1-2), now God was expecting Abraham to give him up? Talk about faith. Abraham trusted God with an unshakeable faith we should strive for every day.

I've never experienced the loss of a child, only witnessed the unimaginable pain of grieving parents. I do, however, know the immeasurable love I have for my children. I've thought of this story many times in regard to my faith. What if God asked me to give up one of my children? Would I willingly agree? I couldn't. It would have to be out of my control. He could ask me to do anything else, and I could probably make it happen. But to sacrifice a child? I couldn't have willingly given up one of mine. Abraham was rock solid faithful. He knew God would not fail him.

Why is it so difficult for us to even have enough faith to endure hardships we face in life? Why is it easy to believe and trust God during the comfortable times, yet so difficult during the trials? God isn't commanding us to sacrifice our children, but He is saying to trust Him. Is that too much to ask of us? We have to be able to come to terms and have peace with a loss of control by handing it over to Him and believing that He wants the best for our life even though it sometimes comes as a result of pain and sorrow.

I am certain that the key to me being able to function at all and still give glory to God, in the midst of my worst pain, is my faith. From the second I knew my husband was no longer breathing, I had no doubt that he was now living in paradise. I have never said "he died," and I understand now why a lot of people don't use that phrase. From my mouth has always come that he "passed away." I've heard others use the phrase that someone "made the transition from this life to eternity." See it has never been in my mind that Chris is dead. He isn't. Sure, his body isn't living anymore. But his soul, the eternal part of him that will never diminish, his soul is living forever, and because of his faith and beliefs in Christ he is now in residence at his *real* home. The one we should all strive to make the journey back to. Thinking of Chris, and that the journey of his life rewarded him with the majesty of Heaven, that was where my mind resided when the pain of grief was overwhelming.

It can't be seen. Someone can't just give it to you. And you certainly can't just go out to the nearest mall and purchase some. The strengthening power and comfort of faith can only come to you through the blood of our Lord and Savior Jesus Christ, by having been on your knees begging for Him to come into your life and save you from yourself, by taking that gift and holding it precious in your heart and mind and soul, by making Heaven your ultimate goal. When Heaven (and eternity there) becomes your focus, the things that don't make sense at all, the most horrific things, will begin to take on new meaning. This life we are living here on Earth is a tiny speck of time compared to what comes next. Life truly is just a vapor, and we are only visitors here—passing through, camping out awhile. We are simply preparing and hopefully sharing, guiding others to that same focus, to that same prize.

We just have to ride this thing out till one sweet day.

I have told the kids many times, "You know dad is just gonna turn around and we'll be there," or "In the blink of his eye, we will be there with him." We talk about how short time is there compared to here and that he's probably saying, "Would y'all stop crying and worrying? You'll be here soon." That is my way of helping them with that focus on eternal things, instead of the experiences here when missing him seems to outweigh everything else.

Like I have said, I had experienced severe losses before losing Chris — especially the unexpected passing of my brother and witnessing the gut-wrenching pain my parents went through in learning to live without their son. I didn't have children at the time, so I couldn't possibly begin to understand, and even still I can't let my mind go there. But I watched as through that horrific time their faith did not give way. It was strengthened. Thoughts of where he was now, and that he was in the peaceful arms of Jesus, is what kept them from completely falling apart. My mom and dad have always been pillars of strength, but I watched them depend on God for strength they couldn't possibly have found alone. Wow, what an amazing example they were to me!

I visibly saw how faith and God's grace work through tragedy. I know that has helped me. More than that, I was raised to have that unwavering kind of faith through difficult times — to not question God, but trust Him fully. I am fortunate to have that rooted in my soul. If that isn't something you are blessed with, pray for it. If you haven't experienced tragedy yet, be thankful, but be prepared. It's coming sooner or later.

And when the tragedy does come, here's what you must accept and find peace in: Being a Christian does not protect you from pain. It prepares you for it. Faith should be a constant in the happy times to be strong enough to withstand the storms. Set your anchor in Christ, the only one who can hold you together when everything around you starts falling apart. If you fully depend on him to get you through, that anchor will hold you safely in his arms. No matter how severe the storm or how many waves of hardship are crashing upon you, you will not sink in the depths of the pain. The pain will still be there, but the difference is this—hope.

Hope is what anchors the soul. It's the only thing stronger than fear. The smallest amount of hope can move mountains. It's the light shining in the dark. Let it come in! Open your heart and allow that hope to heal you from the inside out. You just can't get through a difficult time without it. It will calm your mind, lift your spirit, and carry you to the better days.

And where, oh where, does this hope come from? Jesus of course. The number one comforter, counselor, everlasting Father, light of the world, and Almighty God. Give Him your weakness, and He'll give you His strength. Trust fully in Him, and that hope will have a foundation before the storm hits. Where there is faith, there is hope. Where there is hope, there is light at the end of the tunnel of despair. I have learned to constantly search for the light, always.

It's never too late. Faith is a gift available to us always. God can't force it into our souls, but He is more than willing to flood us with it if only we believe and ask Him and grab hold of it and protect it from the dark. I know for myself, one of my very first goals was to fight the enemy and darkness with what strength I had in me. My faith was my shield and armor and weapon used against what I knew could take me over if I allowed. If I had let my faith waiver, hope could have been unreachable. Joy could have never been found. My children could have lost their mother. I could have lost my soul. That would been a tragedy that no healing could have come from.

I am thankful for my gift. I am thankful that God has made promises that keep my hope alive and have me reaching for that ultimate goal. I hold it dear and precious and will fight until my last breath on this Earth to keep it with me and strive to strengthen it in my soul and share its power with others. And, well, it's also my middle name, so I have a constant reminder and that makes it pretty special. Faith.

Having that faith rooted in my spirit, trusting God and listening to His voice speak to me, is the only way I found hope when the waves of grief seemed to hit me over and over and over again. Oh, how I could have drowned! The word itself sounds painful. Say it out loud. *Grief.* It's often described as deep sadness caused by someone's death. That can't begin to describe the process. Nothing compares. I know of no other experience where so many emotions are being used at the same time, pulling almost every ounce of energy out of you. I'm still in awe of how the human body survives it. Thankfully God gives us the tools we need, if only we pray for the answers of what they are. Again, no instruction manual for reference. And what has helped me might not help you. As I have gone through much of it and prayed for His guidance, God has equipped me with the knowledge of what I needed and still need to heal.

For several months, I remember being exhausted every day to the point I sometimes needed to just lie down and rest my body. Simply *being* is exhausting during grief. Your mind is working overtime to process and accept the knowledge it's been given, while your entire body is in shock and just trying to function in a normal capacity. There's this ongoing battle between truth and desire that you know you can't win, yet your mind continues to fight hoping the truth will change. Consciously you are fully aware nothing will change this new reality. But still, your soul doesn't give up. So the outcome is exhaustion.

The five stages of grief are denial, anger, bargaining, depression, and acceptance. These are in no chronological order, and they most certainly aren't on some linear timeline that we can just check off one by one. In my own experience, they each hung around for a long while at different times, sometimes several at once (exhaustion anyone?) and then sometimes showed up like pop-up showers lasting briefly before they went away again. When I felt relief that I had defeated one train of thought, it would resurface and surprise me again when I least expected it.

For me, denial was the one that consumed me most — not in the sense that I didn't believe the reality. I knew the truth, but my mind struggled for so long adjusting to it. I was past the one-year mark before I could just wake up without having to realize he was still gone. Or I could be doing my day-to-day things and suddenly it would hit me with the same shock. It wasn't intentional. But it happened quite often for some time during that first year, and even into the second. Now as I'm writing this and am in year three, my mind is mostly convinced of this new world we live in, the one without Chris. I no longer need to constantly remind myself. It's still hard to believe that's it's true, and I still sometimes feel like it's a dream. But mostly, my mind has been convinced. It's more settled and calm now. I'm not fighting my reality anymore. I'm still not happy with it, but I have accepted it.

Over the course of my life, I have many times heard about the "power of the mind" and "mind over matter" and various other phrases relating to how powerful the mind is and how you can control so much by the decisions you choose to make. I also believe in being honest and keeping your word, even if it's to yourself. If you decide to do something, do everything possible to accomplish it. That begins by being loyal to the plan and not giving up. Plus, I am very stubborn when it comes to not giving up. That has helped me I'm sure—and the fact that I hate Satan and don't want him to win.

I cannot take credit for positive decisions I made so soon after Chris' passing. I wasn't mentally capable of it. I know without a doubt that God put those thoughts on my heart and mind because He knew if I decided it, I would do everything in my physical power to stick with it. See He knew before I was born that I would one stormy night in June lose my husband, and He knew exactly how I would react to the situation. What I would do. What I would say. He knew it all. Before my first breath. That is so overwhelming and comforting to me. His plan. Not mine.

I look back now and think about the fact that in that car ride home, with my world spinning and logical thought processes nowhere to be found, I began making decisions that would be of great magnitude throughout this journey.

First one: My children would not lose their mother. Ok, obviously no mother would want to be completely different after such a tragic loss, but it does happen. I knew that I would be different of course (how could I not be?), but I made the conscious decision that I would hold onto and give my kids as much of what they knew of me as possible. I decided in that car, while I was more terrified than ever of the life I was instantly thrown into, and physically sick at the thought of what I had to tell our children when I arrived home, that no matter what, I would be recognizable to those children, and I would place them above my own needs. That was God working in me immediately.

Secondly, once we arrived home and the kids and I were sitting on the bed trying to grasp this unthinkable change in our lives, this void that we couldn't comprehend, I heard those words. *Be sure they don't get angry at God.* Again, that was the Lord guiding me in my decisions. By me having that spoken to me and me relaying that message to Averee, Brody, and Lilly, it was being engrained in my mind as well. *Don't get angry with God.* If I had given in to the anger that day in the shower and not been aware of the dangers of it, I could have drowned. I believe when anger is leading you, nothing good follows. Giving in to that desire would have been a dead-end path to emotional and spiritual destruction. I am so thankful that I quickly denied it and told Satan to shut up. He knew from the start that I was going to be a tough one to take advantage of.

Dear Lord, let good come from the situation. Let me see the good and show me the light. I can't handle only darkness and pain. Words can't express what a treasure it is to me that from the early days of losing Chris, I was praying and begging God to show me good and light and blessings and joy. That was my goal every day, to be able to see it. I knew that it was everywhere, but that if I didn't yearn to get even a glimpse of it, I wouldn't. And so I searched for it. Any ounce of it I could find. Every day, with purpose, I prayed that prayer and I kept my eyes wide open to see and receive it. Again, I was determined to not let the enemy win. That kept me focused on battling the darkness with everything in my soul.

In the middle of heartbreak and sorrow, joy will not find you. You will need to search for it, in the simple, beautiful, everyday things. Make it your purpose and ask God to help you have little "happies" to get you through. Even if you only find a speck of joy in the earliest of days, the moments will multiply with time as the sorrow gradually eases up. Find the good, latch onto it, and give yourself permission to be happy. Smile, laugh and embrace each moment. This will not only help drown the pain, it will honor the life of the one you've lost by striving to live each moment in the best way possible.

Don't feel guilty for experiencing fun and being silly. And do not let anyone tell you how to grieve, or worry about what others will think of you. This is your journey to survive, and from experience I can tell you laughter is one of the most amazing and powerful tools within you to heal you and help you move forward. It is possible and likely you will often find joy while still experiencing horrific pain inside. You can genuinely smile on the outside while crying on the inside. It's completely crazy but normal. Some have responded with confused expressions when I've said that I've probably laughed more since Chris' passing than I did before. Not because I'm happier, but because funny things are so much funnier now. Good is that much better. I appreciate much more anything that is the opposite of sadness and pain. I need to be silly, act crazy, and dance and laugh and sing. I need joy. And so, I find it.

It's a decision you must make: let the darkness consume you or escape into the glorious, wonderful, healing power of His light.

Yes, there will be sadness. Yes, there will be undeniable grief and mourning. How could there not be? Tears aren't wasted, and releasing them brings about great relief. They are healing waters created to cleanse the soul one by one. I appreciate every tear that has fallen from my eyes because by them I am changed for the better. I've always felt revived after a complete fall-apart crying session. It's like seeing the sun rays after a rain shower. Soul-reviving. Once they roll out, they are gone forever, and then there is more room for good — and joy.

The balance of it all is not to get lost in the pits of grief. Have a cry, feel the pain, appreciate the healing of it, and then re-focus on the positive. How easy would it have been to get lost in the depths of self-pity during those early days of grief after losing Chris? If I had kept the focus on myself and what I thought I deserved, I would have found myself right back in the direction of anger. Or I would have found myself hiding in the bedroom under the blankets feeling sorry for myself and asking "Why me?" over and over and over again. Did I struggle with the "whys" and "what ifs"? Of course. I'm not saying those thoughts didn't enter my mind. I'm simply saying I didn't allow myself to become consumed with them. I made a conscious decision to fight away any thoughts that I knew weren't from God. That's my only answer as to how I managed to stay more positive than not. It wasn't easy, but nothing good is. You must constantly work at it, like a marriage. But it's the relationship with God that's improving through it. When something happens that you can't fix, you must surrender it all and trust in full reliance of Him. I had never felt so close to the Father as I did once I knew I couldn't possibly function without lots of assistance from Him. Hallelujah that I recognized that's what I needed and still need to get through the bad days knowing the sun will rise and shine again.

Another secret of mine has been learning how to simply *be here now*. Since Chris passed, thoughts of the future have been the most challenging. I can think of the past and smile, but looking ahead brings uncertainty and fear. Once the shock of losing Chris began to wear off, I immediately thought of the life we planned and how it had suddenly exploded out of sight. We are taught as we grow up into young adults to plan and look to the future and be prepared. And then we learn the difficult way that there are occurrences and spans of time that we simply can't prepare for. Death is one of those occurrences. Grief is one of those spans. We can't pen it on the calendar. So, we go through life not thinking about it. We just assume we will start our careers, get married, have babies, and raise them and grow old together. Chris and I had not completed our plan, and the pain of thinking about that was unbearable at first. It didn't work without him. There was no *plan B*. It took quite some time to accept that God will provide me with what I need to finish this revised plan. And so, I learned to focus on right now.

I heard early on to focus on today, and if that's too difficult, focus on this hour, minute, or second. It's the best advice when living through a tremendous loss. I had to teach myself how to immediately shift my focus to what I need to do *right now* to get through the day. I realized if I focused on this moment in time, days and weeks would pass, and over the course of time my heart would be stronger. It worked. Of course I still have to work on it. There are times my mind goes to what could have been, and it still hurts a lot. If I see a movie scene with a dad walking a daughter down the aisle, or I'm at a school function and seniors are being announced and escorted by both parents, I feel dread and sadness.

I've used the same strategy for dealing with thoughts of Chris' accident. When my mind has gone there, I've purposely refocused my thoughts and what needs to be done right now. There were times I might have been running errands and my mind might think of that night, and I would have to literally coach myself: *Ok, Andrea, right now you just have to walk through this parking lot and up to this store. That's all you need to think about right now.*

When the weight of the pain is unbearable, just focus on making it through today. You'll ruin any opportunity to experience an ounce of joy today if you're consumed with fear of tomorrow. Be in control of your thoughts as much as possible. Camp out in the here and now, and be faithful doing all you can do today. Tomorrow has always been uncertain. It's always been out of your control. Just remember: He is already there. Trust in that truth and hold steady — today.

Through my constant reliance on God and witnessing His ever-present work in my life, I have become more and more aware of the power of the Holy Spirit as that presence. When I say God did this or that, spoke to me in this way or carried me through it, I know His Holy Spirit was the presence I felt and witnessed. Before I lost Chris, I didn't acknowledge it as much. It's not that I didn't believe in the Holy Spirit or in its power; it's just that I didn't give it as much credit for the works it had in my life. Now, looking back to experiences I had especially early on, signs that I saw or felt, confirmations I had, comfort and strength that would seem supernatural to unbelievers, it's all confirmation of His presence, that peace that surpasses all understanding, the same peace that Chris was overcome with the week of his passing, the goodness that filled up his last week here, the incredible joyous mood he was in June 5th, the signs from God that He was still good, the unbelievably realistic dreams of comfort that I have experienced. For months after Chris' passing I prayed for a "hug dream." A few months after Travis' accident I had a dream where I saw him at my wedding reception, and we wrapped our arms around each other, and it was so realistic, so comforting. I wanted that dream of Chris. So I prayed and prayed for it, and it never came. Then out of nowhere one night I dreamed that we saw each other and we kissed, and it was the most amazing kiss I had ever experienced. Entirely realistic. I had been praying for the wrong dream! I was limiting my request but was granted something even better. But those type dreams, ones you have to remind yourself are only dreams, I fully believe is the Holy Spirit providing unmistakable comfort when it's needed most, so many blessings bestowed on us during the shakiest storms we endure. It's all works of the Holy Spirit living in us, this treasure that we as Christians are so very blessed with.

We have this incredibly amazing gift available to us without restriction or quantity. The same power that raised Jesus from the dead is living in us. What?! There is no greater power. Why are we not accessing it more? Why do we doubt that it's there? That it's living? That it is still as powerful as it ever was? We all need to pray for it, cry out for it and lay on our face asking God to reveal more and more of this presence to us. I know from experience that He will overwhelm you with His majesty. His grace and mercy. His power. What a gift. A precious, precious gift. The glory of Heaven here with us, shining and showing off its triumph and magnificence. Wow! Just wow! Let that soak into your soul and comfort you like nothing else.

The Holy Spirit has been overwhelmingly present in our lives through this as an answer to many prayers we have prayed. When I have prayed, and have asked others to pray, for comfort, wisdom, strength and peace, I know without a doubt that His Spirit is who provided it. There's no other answer. He hasn't once let me down. I have felt the Spirit working through the pain in unbelievable and unmeasurable ways—goodness all around us and hovering over our home.

God and I are much closer now. I know that's mostly because I work more diligently at that close relationship. He's always in the same place. It is I who is guilty of moving. I do believe in the toughest of times, maybe at our weakest, He pulls us in, if we allow. I know I've never felt closer to Him as the times of my most difficult living.

If you are feeling further from the Lord during a season of pain in your life, pray even if it seems you are just going through the motions at first. Once you take the first step, you will want to pray to Him more and more, as you begin to be aware of the results from it. I believe during these times of trial (and always), there are two forces at work in your life and for your soul — good and evil. Satan wants you as far from God as possible. He wants anger and fear and depression to fill you up and cripple you. He wants you against God at ALL costs, to see Him as the enemy. He wants so much space between you and God so there's more room for him to come in and take over.

God wants you to be filled with light, to be consumed with hope and comfort and peace. He wants to shower you with His grace and mercy, and all He asks is that you accept Him, place your trust in Him, and believe. He wants your dependence on Him because He knows in all our failures, only He can lead us in the path of righteousness and straight up to Heaven.

I have been determined to not give in to the enemy's desires and let him have his way. I refuse to let him win any small victory in my name. I rebuke him and pray in Jesus' name for him to stay clear of me and my children, and our home.

I want good. Always. No matter what. God is good. And everything good comes from God. So, I want God more than anything. Simple solution.

I am so honored and thankful to have shared and passed on

these truths and levels of understanding with the three most important humans in my life, my children. They have also been incredible teachers to me through this walk. More than anything, I've learned the vast amount of faith that exists in a child's heart when they have been taught to believe and can witness the solution it is in coping with loss and grief of this magnitude. I have seen things they have written at school or at church, sometimes speaking of the pain of losing their daddy, but always ending with the same acknowledgement: I know I will see him again. Or they will say, "I'm just happy Dad was a Christian and he's in Heaven." I always reiterate that to him especially around holidays and birthdays. How can you not find comfort in knowing that someone you love is in paradise? Again, just trying to get the focus off us and fixing our eyes on eternal bliss instead of Earthly pain.

I've also learned from observing my three the strength that God gives children through trials and sorrow. What resilience they display! What courage and hope that embody them! I've discovered maybe the fact that they naturally find joy in the right now instead of worrying about the future is a key to some of that. It's such a blessing that I will never take for granted. I remember before Chris passing away, having brief moments maybe during a movie or through seeing someone I know lose a parent or spouse, that I would think *what would happen to our kids if Chris or I passed away?* And then as soon as that vapor of a thought entered my mind, I would shove it back out, just immediately reject that nightmare of a vision. Could not let my mind go there. Just hoped my mind would never have to. And then of course, that nightmare became my life, and as I was faced with that conversation that I prayed was never needed, I was terrified of how our precious children would take the news and be affected by the tragedy that so unexpectedly became our reality. I wasn't prepared to mother children without their father. I didn't have all the answers and to this day I still don't. They are covered up with love and grace, and I always put them and their needs first (which also means I discipline them appropriately), and I try to always help them understand that although it breaks my heart that losing their daddy at such young ages is part of their stories, we are blessed beyond what we deserve, and there are always others who are living more difficult lives.

Are they still affected in negative ways? Are they still missing that father figure that they so desperately need? Are they still sad at times and always needing Chris here? Absolutely. No matter how well they handle this dealt hand, it is always difficult. The sorrow is ever-present, but carefully being controlled by their faith — again, pain and peace residing in the same space.

I realized many months after the accident that Averee, being a teenager and having been older when Chris passed, needed some one-on-one counseling to just get her feelings out without hesitation. Thankfully she welcomed the idea, and was wise enough to realize she needed it, and it has been an amazing tool in helping heal her heart.

It was two years after the accident when I was aware of the need for Brody to go. It was the fourth of July week, and it seemed out of nowhere (grief's best trick) that sadness consumed my little man. The wall of protecting mom, which he had held with all his might, along with his sisters, was crumbling down and true emotion was being revealed. I knew he had not cried enough, talked enough, just faced it enough. And after meeting with the counselor with him, I also realized that his mind was maturing and he was finally able to process his thoughts more like an adult, thus also feeling the pain more like an adult. Lilly's turn came once she was ten, and I saw much healing take place in her in being able to get those feelings out. I'm thankful I have been aware when the stresses of life and pain have become too overwhelming and have recognized what was needed.

Through all of that is another important thing to always remember: Children will do everything in their power to protect those they love the most, even if you tell them not to. It's the good in them. I don't know how many times I said the words, "It's not your job to protect me. It's my job to protect you." I would tell them to cry if they needed and talk to me about anything in their hearts and that I would be ok. And sometimes they would, but most of the time they were afraid of upsetting me. That's what has been amazing about finding the right counselor for them. They don't have to worry about upsetting her. No holding back.

What I've learned that they will let pour out of them is good memories of their daddy. I can bring up *remember when we did this or that, or when your daddy said this or that*, and instantly smiles appear and they engage. We talk about funny things that happened and the bad times as well. I know how important it is to keep reminding them of those memories—all of them—especially for

Lilly who was only six at the time and Brody who was eight. If we continue to re-live those times with Chris, I'm praying it will be engraved in their minds and on their hearts in ways that they can never forget. I learned from my family and especially my parents, you talk about the person. And the more you talk about them and keep their memory alive, the more comfortable you are with doing it and how much it hugs your heart to just simply remember. To remember them is to keep them close to your soul. There is such deep healing in that.

I've learned so much through mothering grieving children, and it is honestly the most difficult thing I've ever done. I grieve deeply for them, as there is nothing worse as a parent than to not be able to *fix* this. It's unfixable. The only option is to help them handle it the best way possible. And then being the mom and the dad, what an overwhelming job! Again, there was no manual to tell me what to do, no directions to read. My only solution was to pray for guidance and wisdom, and think about what Chris would have said or done. The rest has just been God given grace being poured over my head because I fail every day. I get exhausted, I feel inadequate, I feel alone, and I still deal with fear of uncertainty and the future. I know that a lot of that is human nature, and I'm also aware enough of the enemy's power to know he will shove whatever negative thoughts he can in my head. I certainly blame him for them anyway. That gives me an outlet for feelings of anger.

There is a reason the Bible says *do not fear* so many times. There is no peace and calm there. No light. No hope. No comfort. Nothing good comes from fear. When I think about the kids graduating high school or college or weddings or babies or anything special that lies ahead, it's tough. I'm not gonna pretend it isn't. As far as I've come and as much healing that has taken place, it will never be easy to think of anything that he should be here for. Again, there is this new world we are living in where everything else will still happen just as it should and the special events will still take place and the girls will still need someone to walk them down the aisle and Brody will still need someone to teach him all the outdoor things his daddy loved so much, and yet Chris will not be present for any of it, except of course in spirit and in our hearts. I want them to visualize him there during those momentous occasions for comfort and strength. More than any of that, I always try to instill in them that this crazy, difficult life is temporary, the struggles will one day fade away, and they will one day experience the most gratifying momentous occasion of all—seeing him again.

In the midst of the lessons parenting grieving children has taught me, another truth has shown me realizations I could have never possibly been able to grasp while Chris was here. Ok, so obviously I have been surrounded by family and friends and more loved ones than I could ever begin to express my thankfulness for. From early on I was around people all the time, sometimes large crowds of them, but it seemed the larger the crowd, the larger my loneliness felt. I have never experienced that before losing Chris. Maybe some of that was because from the time I was sixteen I was in a relationship. But mostly, Chris and I were each other's halves in the biggest way. We were great compliments to one another, we discussed every aspect of our lives before decisions were made, and we were best friends on top of being in love.

Yes, we had disagreements; of course we made mistakes with one another and sometimes we didn't want to talk to one another because we were caught up in our selfish needs at that moment and weren't putting one another first. We were human after all. But we had a rock-solid marriage and had withstood circumstances and heartaches and hard times that would have crumbled many. We respected one another and never crossed lines that shouldn't be crossed. And we trusted each other as much as one can trust another (there were no passwords on our cell phones). Plus, there was always laughter in our relationship. We had so much fun together. Sometimes it was at my expense, but I didn't care. Chris' laugh was such a gift. If I try hard enough now, I can still hear it.

Losing all those wonderful qualities that complimented me perfectly, it was a punch in the gut. For the longest I had to remind myself not to call him or text, that I didn't need to find out what he wanted for supper or what we should do on the weekend. It wasn't that we spent every waking minute talking or texting or together, but he was here, available and within reach. I missed our occasional Friday night dates without the kids. I missed wrapping my arms around him as soon as he came in the door to just connect one-on-one with him and let him know how much I appreciated him. I missed the vulnerable look in his eyes when he lost someone or something dear to him and when I saw that little boy still living inside of him. I missed the playful times at the beach or the pool or in the yard or him sneaking into the bathroom to pour a cup of cold water on me while I was showering and me screaming to the top of my lungs.

I missed my confidant, my comforter, provider, our family's backbone and strength, my lover. I missed my friend. Every bit of him. The good, the bad and the ugliest of the ugly days we experienced. That's one thing I learned that most don't think about. I would take back the absolute worst day we ever had together over not having him. Not that we had that many bad days (they were rare), but that's not the point. The point is that the entire experience of marriage is beautiful. It's messy and difficult. My goodness, sometimes it is so difficult. There is pain and sorrow and selfish needs and bad moods and screaming kids and dirty diapers and sleepless nights and sicknesses and challenges beyond our imagination when we say "I do." But when you are blessed with a Godly spouse and your marriage is centered around Christ and His commandments and you truly love one another and respect one another and put yourself behind what's needed for the common good, what an amazing gift and journey together it is — this path of hills and valleys that come together in such a beautiful way. To be able to look back and see it all, how magnificent!

It was and still is heartbreaking for me to think about the investment we had in one another and how hard we worked for such a great marriage, and that we won't get to grow old together. We won't be grandparents together and retire and travel like we always talked about. That will always sting. I can't let my thoughts reside in that place too long. However, I wouldn't take back any of it. The good Lord blessed me with fifteen years of memories with

Chris Williamson, a blessed marriage, a supportive extended family, three beautiful children, a home we built together, a church family, amazing friends, and now I'm left with the legacy that he built. If I had known the outcome on January 6, 2001, I still would have said "I do." I wouldn't have changed a thing. The memories in my heart and the smiles they bring are worth the pain. And yes, if I could go to that back yard on June 5, 2014 around 7:30 p.m. and force him to get in my car and bring him home and keep him safe from harm, of course I would. I would trade every blessing and every ounce of good that has come from the tragedy of our lives to have him back. But, since that's not an option and I trust in the Lord's plan as a greater one of difficult understanding, I find peace in leaning on Him and looking ahead to eternal gain instead of Earthly satisfaction.

Will I one day find love again and experience the same kind of relationship that my heart so desperately misses? Will my kids ever be able to have a father figure (not a replacement) that is such a void in their lives? If the Lord so sees fit. If I ever look at someone and don't automatically think *that isn't Chris*, or if I know without a shadow of a doubt that someone will bless our lives and make them better or with more ease, then yes, maybe it will happen. I know God blesses our lives with love because it enriches the experiences of life. But I put my trust in His plan and His timing. I will know when or if that special someone comes along. I'm not going to go out searching for it. I have three children that take up so much of my time and focus that it would have to be a person of complete respect and admiration for me to invest in. When that person comes along, I won't even hesitate or have doubts or wonder how my time or energy could be divided. It won't matter. God will give me peace with it and it will just be—easily and without fear, knowing it is blessed by God and that Chris would bless it as well.

Will I ever stop loving Chris or remembering our life together? Not a chance. Will that person have to be able to accept that I will always have those feelings, but will not be limited by them? Absolutely. Chris will always have an ever-present place in my heart and mind, and I will bring up his name to my children when I see fit and that will just have to be ok because that is what's important. I will never compromise my beliefs and priorities with regards to my faith or love for my children and their well-being for anyone.

Knowing that each of us yearns for the blessing of love and companionship and comfort and support in the form of an Earthly relationship, I have also been taught through my experience that we mustn't rely on it for happiness. We cannot judge our value on whether we have it. I, not having that relationship for almost three years as I type these words, have learned that my true happiness in life must first and foremost come from my Father in Heaven and His purpose for my life. I must place my complete and unwavering reliance on Him, look to Him first for comfort and strength and have a successful relationship there, and anything else is just a bonus to help in these temporary day-to-day experiences. I know God wants us to experience the joy and contentment that comes from love, but until He is the center of our lives, we still won't be truly happy and content. We will always be searching for something, not knowing what we're missing, unless we have that successful relationship with God first.

I am in constant works with my relationship with Him, knowing I am far from where I need to be, but my understanding of what I need more than anything else (God), overflows into realizing that I don't "have to" have a romantic relationship. I miss it, and of course it would enrich my life, but it is not what determines my happiness.

I've learned that finding peace in the storm of losing Chris, losing the love of my life, my children losing their father, the pain our family has endured from the tragic loss, especially his parents, it's a result of seeking and receiving the Lord's presence in my life with complete faith and trust in Him and His infinite wisdom. Once I start asking *why* and *what if* and *how come* and on and on with the questions, I lose focus on the fact that even if He gave me the answers, my simple human mind wouldn't be able to truly comprehend and understand the depths of His ultimate plan. It wouldn't change the wanting and the missing and the wishing. I am anxious for the day when all the knowledge and reasoning are revealed and my eyes are completely and clearly opened to see it all and have those answers. For now, I find peace in believing what my eyes cannot see, knowing the truths that He has given me for guidance, and setting my eyes on the prize of finality that awaits me on that glorious, wonderful day. What a day that will be, when my Jesus I shall see. When all the glory of Heaven is revealed and the story is understood and the majesty of paradise is opened up and I set my eyes on the Father. Knowing that this pain, this yearning, this void that we feel, it's temporary, and remembering that Chris no longer has our troubles, our sorrows, our worries, it gives me joy when joy is hard to find.

"Blessed be the God and Father of our Lord Jesus Christ! According to His great mercy, He has caused us to be born again to a living hope through the resurrection of Jesus Christ from the dead, to an inheritance that is imperishable, undefiled, and unfading, kept in Heaven for you, who by God's power are being guarded through faith for a salvation ready to be revealed in the last time. In this you rejoice, though now for a little while, if necessary, you have been grieved by various trials, so that the tested genuineness of your faith- more precious than gold that perishes though it is tested by fire- may be found to result in praise and glory and honor at the revelation of Jesus Christ. Though you have not seen Him, you love Him, you believe in Him and rejoice with joy that is inexpressible and filled with glory, obtaining the outcome of your faith, the salvation of your souls."

–1 Peter 1:3-9

Chapter 8
MY PRAYER

So now what? I carry on with the same plan I have had since the night my world flipped upside down June 5, 2014. I pray. A lot. It may simply be a conversation when I'm driving down the road, a statement I make as I'm getting dressed on Sunday for church, still missing picking out his clothes for him, or it may be a long teary-eyed plea as I lay down alone at night needing more wisdom and guidance than ever before. And sometimes it's just me saying, *Thank you Lord for blessing us the way you have. Thank you for holding me up and carrying me through and helping me to better days.*

But I pray because I do not want to lose focus. I do not want to become complacent and content in where I am spiritually. I do not want it to take another tragedy to make me more dependent on Him because I never want to become independent from Him. And in those prayers of asking Him to lead, guide and direct me, I pray that I stay minded in the here and now, not worrying or in fear about the future, but finding joy in each moment God is blessing me with in this beautiful life. I pray that I always search for the good and the light and every speck of happiness that is available for my taking because I know the good Lord wants it for me. Every funny thing I experience or crazy moment of embarrassing my kids when

I don't act my age, I pray I cherish those moments and keep my spirit light and joyous, realizing that my moments are limited and life truly is a vapor.

With every ounce of my being I will strive to be the good in this world and do what Chris did by sharing what Christ has done for me and my kids and to find every opportunity to help others in need and lift the spirits of the struggling. I pray that the healing in my heart and in the hearts of my children and all our family continues a steady path and that we continually grow closer through the appreciation we have more now of knowing tomorrow may never come for either one of us.

I pray that I always remember to keep my focus—first on the Lord, and my children, and us striving to increase our kingdom works daily. I pray that I remember in my worst day to focus on the hour or minute or second, whatever my heart can bear at the time to get me through it, knowing I have survived much worse days and I can conquer it too with Him backing me every step (or crawl) of the way. I pray that I always focus on the one true solution to any problem I face, and know that through Him anything truly is possible.

I pray that I always find joy, even in the worst of days, because that is when the joy is the most precious and valuable. The sun is so much more appreciated after the rain. Without the rain, that bright warm sunlight would be so taken for granted. Just as in our lives, if everything was great and without pain, what would we need God for? If life on Earth was only filled with happiness and good, would we strive for Heaven as much? I don't think so. I know

I have never strived as much for Heaven as I have now. There is so much precious to me there. I am invested in my ticket to that promised land. I want my name called on that day. With Heaven as my focus and knowing my purpose is to be a witness to what God has carried me through with the power of the Holy Spirit, I can get through my days here with peace and anticipation. I'm making the most of my time while I look ahead to the reward we as Christians strive for, the reward Chris strived for, the reward he is experiencing now. I pray I never forget that.

I pray every day that my children are being taught the lessons that will enrich them the most and that any speck of wisdom I can pass on to them is being imprinted on their minds. I pray they look back one day and remember me as a warrior for Christ and as a warrior for them. I pray that they remember smiles and laughs more than tears and pain. I pray that they remember every time I placed their needs above my own. I pray that my faith and trust in Him is being passed on to them the same way it was passed on to me.

With tears in my eyes and pain in my heart, I pray they remember their daddy. I pray they remember the love he had for them — the unselfish, unconditional, full of pride and acceptance and respect and support, biggest and without reservation love his heart exploded with for them. I pray they remember his hazel eyes and long eyelashes and the scar on his left eyebrow and his strong callused hands that worked so hard for us and his broad shoulders and tan skin and his infectious laugh and southern voice that loved to sing and the way he loved watching them do anything. I pray they remember that everything he did was with them and me as the top priority and how he only wanted our lives to be easier and happy.

I pray they understand how much it pained him to even think he might miss a ballgame or church service or school program or holiday because of work. I pray that they know any extra hours he ever worked were only to make our lives easier. He would have given it all up before he ever let it get in the way of his relationship with us. I pray that they know that he would have never chosen to have left us. Not in a million years.

I also pray that they truly believe their daddy was a great man. I pray they know he is respected because he was respectful, he is honored because he was honorable, and he is loved because he loved. He invested himself in what matters most in this life, his relationship with God, his family, and in others. He didn't care if his name was famous or if his bank account was full. The center of this wonderful man was the Lord and his family. That was where his most successes were found. That made him happy. His legacy speaks for itself. I am so proud.

I pray that Averee and Brody and Lilly grow up carrying on the legacy that their daddy left. I pray that they stay centered and focused always knowing the pride he had and still has for them and the deep admiration and respect I have for them having watched more strength and resilience in them than I've witnessed in most adults. I pray that they know they always have a daddy, that is living more than any of us, and preparing to see them again. I pray they keep striving to get to that place one day, to see his face and that big smile beaming on his face as he lays his Heavenly eyes on his biggest Earthly treasures again. Oh, it makes me explode with happiness to think about! Chris and Jesus and all our loved ones! One sweet day! I can't wait.

I pray that everything in my mind and my heart that has been changed for the better resulting from the terrible pain I've endured stays changed for the better. I pray I keep changing for good. Every second of every minute of every day while I still have a breath in my lungs and a beat in my heart, I pray I grow and learn and increase in trust and faith and boldness and that I continue to let go of the control I think I have. I pray that I remember to lean on Him who is in control and that I remember when life gets to be too much to simply *be still*.

I pray that I never forget: The life Chris and I shared. Every moment of it. The good, the bad, the happy and sad. The moment I knew I loved him. The second our eyes met on our wedding day. His kiss. His strong embrace. How safe I felt in his arms. How happy he made me. I pray that I never forget the excitement in his voice when those three pregnancy tests were positive. How he would have had more kids without hesitation because he loved the chaos and craziness of it all because it was our life and it made him overflow with happiness. I pray I never forget how proud he was to be my husband. That he saw me at my absolute worst physically and emotionally and he loved me the same either way. That he always told me I didn't need makeup. I pray that I never forget his voice. How he said "I love you, Andrea." How he made me feel. I pray I never forget the sacrifices he made. Of his time, his energy, sleep. Everything he gave up to serve in his profession. I pray I never forget the physical wear on his body from going and going and going and never complaining. I pray the appreciation for what he did for us never goes away. I pray that I always honor him and do everything in my power to remember him and keep his memory close. I pray I never forget. Any of it. Ever.

Lastly I pray I never give up. I pray that the stubbornness God placed in my spirit remains and that the fire within me has flames that never can be extinguished. I pray I constantly stay on the positive path, knowing there will be sadness and disappointments, but that as I have gotten through the worst of this, I can come out on the other side of any challenge I face in this life. I pray that I never get angry at God. That I always defeat the enemy. And that I remember where my strength and comfort and peace come from. I pray that I only look back to experience the memories and lessons, not with regret or remorse.

I pray that I always share my story. Chris' story. God's story. I pray that I always remember what He has done for me, undeserving and sinful me. I pray that I remember His grace and mercy that covers me and washes me clean, that I am His and He is proud. I pray that I can look back at the end of my life and see the beautiful way it all came together, through the sun and through the storms, seeing how He sheltered me always.

I pray that I remember He carried me — every time I asked and even when I didn't. He knew what I needed and provided when I didn't deserve. I pray that my life is filled with joy and happiness and comfort and peace and that when the bad times come and the waves cover my head, I will never forget to hold His hand and beg for His presence always.

I pray I can always say, *I love You Lord. You alone are my refuge. My strength. My comfort. My peace. You are all knowing. You have my best interest at heart. You want joy in my life. You are the answer for everything. You hold me up when I cannot stand, and You wrap your arms around me when my world is too much to bear. You know my heart. And my pain. You know my past and my future, and You cherish me no matter what. You are my Father. I am your child. Your love surpasses everything. For that alone, I trust You. Like a child to a parent. I hand it all over to You. I surrender my wishes and wants to You, and I follow You Lord. Lead me in this life. Guide me on the path. I will never doubt. I will never give up. I am always Yours. I lay at Your feet humble and broken and say here I am Lord. Let Your will be done. I will always love You. I will always trust You. I will always look to You. For everything. I will always remember what You have done for me that I have never deserved. That I sometimes didn't have the wisdom or strength to ask for. But still. You were there. You still are. Forever and always. The beginning and the end. The first and the last. The Almighty God. King of the world. Comforter. Provider. All-knowing. All-loving. Gracious and merciful. My strength. My guide. Unconditionally loving me and all my flaws and forgiving me over and over and over again because of the sweet name of Jesus. As long as I live and for the rest of eternity, I'll never forget, Lord. I'll never forget. Thank you, Father, for everything. It can never be enough, but thank You.*

"I will give thanks to the Lord with my whole heart; I will recount all of your wonderful deeds. I will be glad and exult in You; I will sing praise to Your name, O Most High."

–Psalm 9:1-2

"Rejoice always, pray without ceasing, give thanks in all circumstances; for this is the will of God in Christ Jesus for you."

–1 Thessalonians 5:16-18

"Make a joyful noise to the Lord, all the Earth! Serve the Lord with gladness! Come into His presence with singing! Know that the Lord, He is God! It is He who made us, and we are His; we are His people, and the sheep of His pasture. Enter His gates with thanksgiving, and His courts with praise! Give thanks to Him; bless His name! For the Lord is good; His steadfast love endures forever, and His faithfulness to all generations."

–Psalm 100

"Oh give thanks to the Lord; call upon His name; make known His deeds among the peoples! Sing to Him, sing praises to Him; tell of all His wondrous works! Glory in His holy name; let the hearts of those who seek the Lord rejoice! Seek the Lord and His strength; seek His presence continually!"

–Psalm 105:1-4

Chapter 9
THREE YEARS

June 5, 2017.

As I sit in the Wesley Chapel cemetery looking at the headstone with his name, our children's names, my name, the dates with the dash that never get easier to look at, I am reflecting. It's difficult to take my mind back. It feels like a knife when I do. But it's important. Feeling glimpses of that sorrow and pain remind me of how far I've come, how far He has brought me. Remembering that nightmare of a day three years ago, it makes me cherish the good days—days before that phone call, when our family and life were as they should be, when there was a mom and a dad and three children in a happy and safe home and environment with faith and love and respect and laughter and joy, when we felt we had finally gotten to an *easy* or at least easier life, when our stresses were few and our memories were those of happiness and fun and as simple as they were, more important than anything in this world.

I think back to that day. I remember so much and then not enough. I remember more than anything the smiles I could hear in his phone calls and the hearing "I love you" and the complete void of worry that was in me. The outcome of that day was so unexpected. So out of nowhere. So unwelcomed. Never anticipated. When he left our house late that afternoon, I expected to see him pull back in. It might have been the next morning when everyone had gotten their power back on, it might have been him returning exhausted and soaking wet and dirty, but still I expected him back home.

When he sat down to eat with us before he left, I expected many more meals with him at that kitchen table, more blessings together, more laughs, more shared day-to-day experiences, more cleaning up together, just more. When he kissed me goodbye and I told him "be careful," I never expected it to be the last. I never thought about it once. I expected more affection and more comfort and more embraces and more love to make up the rest of our lives together. I expected more dirty clothes and more dirty boots and more dirty dishes and more of everything.

If I had only known, I would have done so much more. I would have told him more, my appreciation for him and how he provided for us, his willingness to put us first and himself second. If I had only known, I would have said "I love you" ten times as much, so much he would have been sick of it, just because I did and do love him that much. I would have put him above me more. I would have listened more intently and with more support and encouragement. I would have picked up after him more, instead of getting angry when I felt he should have done it. I would give anything now to pick up after him, to do anything for him.

If I had only known, I would have praised him more. I would have told him more what an amazing Christian man he was and how much his smile lit up a room and how his laugh could never be duplicated because it was that incredible. If I had only known, there is no limit to what I would have given up to add one more smile to his beautiful face, to make his life easier, to focus more on him and less on myself. If I had only known, I would have prayed with him more. On our knees. Giving thanks to God every day for the amazing life he had blessed us with. If I had only known.

I wouldn't take any of it back. I wouldn't change it. If I had only known, I would still have married him. I would still have built a life with him. I would still have done it all because it was worth the pain and anguish my heart has felt. The vast amount of love in my heart for Christopher Lane Williamson is the reason my heart still and always will have a hole. But, the dance of life that we shared, goodness it was amazing while it lasted. For a moment, all in our world was right. We couldn't have known. It's a blessing we didn't. It would have crippled us to have known. And so, God knows the best way.

Still, I miss my friend, the one my heart and soul confided in about everything, the man I felt the safest with, the one person in my life whose comfort I have needed the most. The one who could have made me feel better more than anyone else has. I have just needed his hug. Him holding me saying, "It's gonna be alright, Andrea." And so, the pain always remains. Time does help, adjustments are accepted, and my mind learns more and more every day that this indeed is real and is my life now. I still have moments when I have a hard time believing it, when I still want to change it, to wake up and forget this terrible dream.

My hope comes from knowing I will indeed see him again. June 5th wasn't the end. Not at all. When my heart is breaking, when hope seems lost, I stay strong and I keep holding on because I know this is true. I look forward to that reunion more than anything. I hold steady and focused because I want what Chris has — the same reward.

When I reflect on these three past years, I am thankful. Thankful isn't even a strong enough word. Neither is appreciation. Overwhelmed is probably the best description of how I feel. Frank told us all on June 9th at Chris' service that it wasn't the last time to pay respects to him. People listened. I have lost count of the times he has been honored and shown respect to since the accident. I have lost count of the gifts that have been given to me and the kids, texts of encouragement, phone calls, cards in the mail, donations to charities, the list is never-ending. I can never repay it. I can never say thank you enough. I just pray that people know my gratitude and respect for them.

The guys at the Florence Electricity Department cooked breakfast for us this morning and prayed with us and visited with us because they are respectable men who respected Chris and continue to show respect to him and our family over and over again because they want to and because he meant a lot to them and was also their family. After all, he spent as much time with some of them as he did with us. They loved each other. They looked out for each other. Chris was blessed by them. And now we are. What a gift!

As I reflect, I see covering all of it, showering down

cleansing the pain out tear by tear, the love of Christ—the One responsible for any healing, any growth, any ounce of anything good in this crazy, difficult life. I see Him carrying me, wrapping His arms around me like I asked Him to—and still do—especially in the worst of days. I know He is the reason when I fell I got up, when I was broken He put me back together, when I doubted He confirmed. When I needed Chris back more than anything in the world, He showed me that Chris isn't far. He showed me that I could withstand the pain if only I depended fully on Him and His word. He was always the answer. The good and light came only from Him. For that I will always praise Him and His holy name. I will always tell others He is my strength. Because of what He has done in my life, I will find more than ten thousand reasons to sing and hold His name on high. I will remind myself every day that He is the king of the world—for me not to understand, but for me to respect and love and follow and worship. Always.

And when that sweet, glorious day comes, oh I truly can only imagine what will be in store for me. I can only imagine the magnitude of joy filling that infinite space and hearing the Lord say "well done." I can only imagine because it's so much more magnificent than our human eyes and minds could ever try to vision. But I am excited for that day. That's where my happiness lives and reigns. That's where peace is found and that's where every tear will be wiped from our eyes and we will see the glory of Heaven in all its splendor and know it was all worth it. Everything—the pain, the disappointments, the suffering, the losses, the grief we all must experience while living this life. All gone, all wiped clean, all just stepping stones leading us back to our Father.

For now, I will rest easy in that thought. I will carry it with me always. I will take this life one day at a time and I will tell the good news that is for all to hear. I will find joy and laughter and fun in every day because I want to experience life so much more now. I will listen to the birds sing and the wind blow and watch ocean waves and stare at the stars with more wonder and cherish it more than ever before because I don't want to miss a second. I will dance and sing and laugh with my kids and show them that joy is always available, that every emotion and every experience, good or bad, it's all so important. I will look back with no regrets and no remorse, knowing although I will fail and I will stumble and fall many times through my life, I will always rise, with unwavering faith.

I will continue to see God's plan as perfect, even when I can't see the *why* and when I don't agree. I will continue to depend on Him always, for everything and to look to Him for guidance and wisdom and strength, to know He is always good. Always. At the end of my life, when this is all just a memory and a story to tell, I hope I will always say and believe the words that are so difficult to accept but so sweet to say —

It is well with my soul.

The following are thoughts of my children following the three-year anniversary of Chris' accident:

>*Three years. How has the time gone by so quickly? It seems like it all happened last week. Every word, every sound, every minute from those awful days are still fresh on my mind. For the past week or so, I've thought about this day on repeat. How it changed me, how it changed my family, and how it changed my life. It completely flipped my life around to where I didn't have a normal anymore.*

>*If there is anything that I've learned from all this heartache, it's this – If God has brought you this deep into the troubling waters, He's not going anywhere any time soon. Also, nothing can grow without a little rain storm. We have to go through troubling times such as this to grow stronger, that's life. We can't change just by doing the same thing over and over. Just to think about all of this breaks my heart, because I'm still going through this. You can't ever get through all of it, but you go through it every day.*

>*I miss dad so very much, but in the end I wouldn't change anything that happened in the past three years. Even though the following days are awful memories, I wouldn't choose to forget them. They made my family and me stronger and closer. I wouldn't trade them for anything. And who am I to wish my dad was back here on this terrible earth, while he's partying it up in Heaven? I'm no one to wish that. These past three years of my life have been a growing and life*

changing experience that will never fade. But it's all worth it in the end, I know that for a fact. When I hear God say "well done good and faithful servant" to me, I'll smile and remember that this heartache, sorrow, grief and pain will always be okay. It'll always be worth it in the end.

–Averee Williamson

I've learned that life can change in the blink of an eye and to tell the people you love how you feel while you have the chance to.

–Brody Williamson

I've learned to be brave and not be afraid for the things ahead.

–Lilly Williamson

EPILOGUE

It was about a year after Chris passed. Lilly and I were on the back deck of our house, enjoying a beautiful Alabama evening, and she had just finished dancing lyrically for me which she did from time to time. She went back inside and I enjoyed some quiet time in thought and prayer.

Overwhelming feelings of loneliness came about, and my mind wondered to a place it was very familiar with—a place where I longed for something that also terrified me. I began to pray.

Lord, this feeling is hard. I need the relationship that I'm missing so badly. I know I can't have it with Chris anymore, but I need it—the comfort and happiness and security that only come from that. But I'm scared, Lord. I'm scared to think of it: the possible complications, how it would affect the kids, everything. I know that I'm not yet ready, Lord, and it may never be Your will for me to have it again. But, Lord, I pray that it is. I pray that You can bless me and the kids with someone amazing who will love us and take care of us and who will wrap his arms around me and give me the comfort that no one else here can. Please, Lord, if it be Your will, please let me have that again.

I've heard people say they heard God speak to them. I admit

I always wondered what that was like before I experienced it. I had never asked for it enough or been open to it enough until Chris passed. And after getting my heart and soul in the right place for it, I heard God speak to me several times. But that summer evening, it was as clear as I had ever experienced.

Be patient.

I heard it several times. It was like God knew I might brush it off if He didn't repeat Himself. It was simple and to the point and there was no room for question or confusion or misunderstanding. *Just be patient? That's it? That's all I need to do? I can do that, Lord! Be patient. I got it.*

I'm not saying I heard God's actual voice. What I heard was a message in my mind, in my voice, but from Him. There was no doubt that it was Him.

The Lord knows patience isn't easy. It's such a simple yet difficult quality to possess—to just wait. We want to do things when we want to do them and we want to get things when we want to get them. We live in a world where we don't have to be patient. If we want something that we don't have, well we just go out and get it. Immediate gratification is more common than not.

Something I've learned that I hope to pass on is that pure, true love that is God-blessed comes in His time, not ours. He knows what's best for us and when it's best for us. We're so accustomed to hearing how we decide our lives and our fates and our experiences and our relationships—and of course God gives us freedom—but we often forget that ultimately He is in control. If we listen to His voice and follow His will for us, He will deliver what we need in His time, not ours.

When He spoke to me that night, I knew that was what I had to do. And I did. For months and months and months and months I was patient. Anytime I wished for someone or prayed for someone or went anywhere where there were couples and I felt out of place or I was just tired from being a single parent, I (and God) reminded myself—*be patient*.

I never had the desire to hurry and find someone or go out looking for that. I knew in the depths of my soul God would send me the one I was praying for. I knew when the time was right and my heart had healed enough and the kids were at a place they could welcome another man into their lives, God would provide. He had told me what to do and I was doing it and although it was sometimes a difficult thing—waiting—I did.

During this time of waiting—and after suggestions and lots of prayers and soul-searching moments and doubts and fears being pushed aside by my God—I started writing this book. What a healing process it was. This book was my counselor a lot of days and late nights. Typing through tears cleansed my soul in ways I never imagined. There were days I dreaded it, just didn't want to go to the place of pain I had to go, but still, I did.

After I had been writing for a few months maybe, if my

thoughts went to that place again — the one where I longed for a new love — I heard a new command along with *be patient* — *You've got to finish the book.* Honestly finishing something of this magnitude seemed way more difficult than just waiting. Waiting was mostly easy for me. Writing my worst pain was at times the hardest task imaginable. But, God said do both, so I did.

I knew in my heart that if I met someone during the time I was writing the book, it would be more difficult to stay focused on it. Not because I wouldn't want to, but because if I had something new come into my life that brought joy and laughter and comfort that I had missed so much, it would be very difficult to get my mind back to that pain. I'm not saying that a new love would make me forget Chris or my experience of losing him, but it would have been more difficult to put myself back into that mindset. It just would have.

Knowing that God was leading me to get this complete, I stayed focused on it, and I focused on letting Him heal me and I focused on being the best mom I could be and to help the kids heal as much as I could.

During this time of waiting and writing, I found as much joy as possible. The kids and I had fun experiences and laughs and made wonderful memories and went on vacations and simply learned to make the best out of our new lives. There were still days we just got through and the pain was more prevalent and life was hard and he was missed ALWAYS, but we could always see the sun through those cloudy (and sometimes stormy) days.

I learned over and over through the grief of losing Chris and adjusting to the new life I was living, my focus had to be in the moment. I had to keep my mind on what joy I could find right then, and just live. Satan is a master at trying to manipulate our minds into focusing on fearful thoughts. I fought hard against that and reminded myself often to focus on now. I promise it was a God-sent gift to be able to do that most of the time.

June 5, 2017, I was determined to "finish" the book. I went to the cemetery that afternoon with that goal in mind. And I wrote *Three Years* believing it was the last I would write. Since then I have decided to add these thoughts, because listening and trusting the Lord has rewarded me and richly blessed my life and I want to give Him glory and praise for the new chapter in my life.

At the cemetery that day after an hour-and-an-half of reflecting and writing (and lots of ugly crying), I felt led to post a video of me reading those words on Facebook. As always, I was given an enormous amount of encouragement and kind words and hopefully me doing that did what I hoped it would — give others a perspective that can only come through tremendous loss. I have always prayed since that tragic day in June 2014 for God to use me for good. Hopefully being able to openly share my experiences and feelings have been for His good purpose.

After reading and rereading and rereading these chapters so many times I didn't know if my words made sense at all, I trusted a friend with the task of editing my grammar and I felt a huge relief to just have it out of my hands and mostly off my mind for a while. I went back to just living, and it seemed after we hit that three-year mark the healing came more quickly and tears were shed less frequently. What a relief.

We were in the busyness of plans for the 2017 Chris Williamson Wild Game Fest, the kids started back to school, and life was what I had grown accustomed to. The familiarity of our family dynamic kept me comfortable, but the thoughts were in the back of my mind—*I finished the book, Lord. Now what?*

August 22, 2017, a normal Tuesday night at the Williamson household. I randomly got a message on messenger from a lady I didn't know. What's weird and wonderful at the same time is the opening of her message was that she had messaged me after my husband's passing and that her husband is a lineman. I immediately scrolled up to see that yes, she had messaged me the day after Chris' accident, and I had responded much later once I saw the message. She said she had been added to our Impulse Boutique VIP group page on Facebook and had then looked at my personal profile and watched the video I posted at the cemetery. She said *I prayed over you and your babies.* If you've gone through something tragic as a Christian, you know the significance of those words.

I suppose the next part of her message would seem crazy to a lot, but as believing as I am in the power of the Holy Spirit and how God gives us messages, I was truly open to what she had to say.

She proceeded to tell me that after watching the video and crying and praying for us, that for some reason every time my boutique posts showed up in her newsfeed, she immediately thought about her (and her husband's) friend Darron. She told me some about his background and his kids. And then she said *he is a GREAT GUY. God-fearing. Southern gentleman. To his core.* She had seen him that night at a school event and told him how she couldn't stop thinking about why he would pop in her head when she saw my Impulse posts. She told him what she knew about my situation and showed him my picture. He later told me he thought she was crazy, and he wasn't looking for anything romantic at the time, but when he saw my picture he couldn't help but look at my profile. He had texted her and said he watched the video of what I posted at Chris' grave and that he would absolutely love to meet me. He said *someone like her is a rare find.* I do agree that I'm different on a lot of levels, but I don't agree with what Darron said because I don't think highly of myself at all. However, hearing that he said that about me after watching that video — something very raw and real and overall sad — something that would scare away most men — it touched my heart in so many ways at the kind of person this man must be.

She ended the message with that she knew it was awkward and weird and she didn't know where my heart was and that I didn't know her from anyone, but that she just had to let our names cross.

I responded carefully to her that I would be happy to get to know him a little and that I might be at a place where my heart would be ready, if God saw fit.

The next morning—a Wednesday—he sent me a friend request, and I accepted. The day went on and we went to church that night to meet with final plans and stay after to set up tables and chairs in preparation for the Saturday Wild Game Fest event. We were finishing up and getting ready to leave when I received a messenger notification. A message from Darron Hood. I waited until we were home and settled in before I opened it and was quickly impressed. He obviously wasn't trying to pick me up or just take me out. He first said he hoped he wasn't bothering me or overstepping boundaries and then introduced himself to me and gave his condolences for what had happened. He said he watched the video I posted and that he could tell by the way I talked that Chris and I were a very blessed couple, and that it was evident God had His hand on me through all of it, and that he would be praying for me and the kids.

A woman knows when she's being hit on even if the exact words aren't said. I didn't feel that at all from Darron. He genuinely just wanted to get to know me without pressure or expectations. I could feel that immediately from him. And he wanted me comfortable no matter what. From the beginning Darron would always say *whatever you're comfortable with* or *I hope I'm not bothering you*. Always very polite, very sensitive to me and my needs, and it was evident that he was just GOOD.

We texted and talked on the phone for a few weeks, and then on September 7, 2017, met for the first time for dinner. To say I was a nervous wreck is a mild description. I hadn't been on a first date since I was twenty-years-old. I had no idea what to expect and how to do the whole dating thing, if I even wanted the whole dating thing, and all I can say is bless his heart! I have since told Darron he was the best man for the job of dealing with me on that first date, because I could tell he understood the process of *starting over* and the feelings that come with it. As weird as it sounds, I felt like I was being unfaithful to Chris, even after three years.

Darron and I talked through dinner and walking a few blocks to the parking lot and ended the night with a few hugs and a lot of apologies from me for just being so nervous. I felt like I had not been myself and couldn't just see him for who he was instead of worrying so much. He texted after we both made it home with the sweetest message. And through all the fear and worry in my head of the unknown, the one certainty was that I wanted to continue to get to know this man better because I felt a connection to him that comforted my heart.

We continued to text and talk into the next week and he asked me to go out on his boat with him on that Friday, and I agreed. We met again, and I arrived at the boat ramp parking lot before him. I prayed until that man pulled up. *Please Lord let me be*

myself. Please take away the nervousness and the worry and just let me be
me. Lord, please let me see Darron for who he is. Let me just look at him
and see his heart and the man he is and just be myself.

Darron pulled up a few minutes later, I got out of my Tahoe as he was getting out of his truck, and he told me later that when he saw me that night he knew I was ok. We spent hours on the boat talking. He fished some and I sat there and just watched him almost with a new set of eyes. I did see him for who he was that night and I was much less nervous. It seemed that just me and Darron (and a lot of praying) was what I needed. No distractions, no worrying about who might see me out on a date for the first time, no expectations. Just us. We talked for a while once we got back to the truck, said goodnight, and I left completely different than I had left the week before.

In previous conversations with friends, I had said two things would have to happen for me to ever have another romantic relationship again: I would look at the man and not think, "That isn't Chris," and it would have to be something I wouldn't be able to fight against, because I knew I would fight against it if I could. I had grown so accustomed to our new way of living, and I finally knew how to do life again—just me and the kids. Change is scary, so I knew I would try and fight any feelings that brought change. With Darron, I never looked at him and compared him to Chris, except to see some of the same characteristics that would be required of a man in mine or my kids' lives. I did try and fight my feelings some with nervousness and fear of complications, but I just couldn't not have Darron in my life. I didn't want a life without him in it.

The next three months were spent getting to know each other more, introducing each other to our kids and our kids to one another. So many words were texted, so many phone conversations, so many laughs, so many (good) tears, so many date nights, so many wonderful memories with our kids of hiking and nights around the fire pit and card games and nighttime hide and seek.

We fell completely in love. I don't even feel like I fell. I feel like this door opened and I walked in and immediately knew I was home. What an incredible feeling—receiving a gift from God that you prayed so many prayers for but realizing your expectations weren't near as high as what He provided. *Goodness* is the best response my mind and heart has.

December 23, 2017. Darron and the kids were coming out to our house to exchange gifts and have breakfast for dinner. I asked him if we wanted me and him to exchange one of our gifts with the kids all together and he said that would be good. After dinner and letting the kids open theirs, I gave him a new wallet I had gotten him and then he handed me my box. It felt very light! I opened the box to find—nothing. He said, "Oh I forgot to put it in there," and got down on his knee and held up a box with a beautiful symbol of love and asked me to marry him right there in front of our babies. Nothing could have been more perfect. I said *yes* through the happiest of tears and we embraced and our kids were excited and at that moment the word *hope* became very real again.

Darron and I are now planning a life together with our kids, and the love that we feel is overwhelming and it grows more every day. It truly is amazing. I know our experiences have made us so much more appreciative and have shaped us into the people we are as God was preparing us for each other. We are living a life that is much different than what we planned several years ago, but God is good and so is this life.

Looking back at my mindset before I met Darron, it was so difficult to see how I could ever truly be happy with someone again. How I could ever trust someone with my heart and with my kids. How I could start a new life again and not be fearful of the unknown and the what-ifs. It was impossible to visualize it. But those prayers, the prayers I poured out to the Father over and over asking Him to send what I had difficulty believing would ever happen, they were answered with a magnitude of blessings I have no words for. I asked and the Lord said, *But I'll give you more.* And He did. He has blessed me with the best twice. What a gift!

Seeing how God's plan brought me to where I am spiritually, emotionally and in my relationship with Darron and others, I can only imagine the eye-opening experience of Heaven. To be able to see how every experience, good and bad, shaped us and led us to exactly where He planned us to be from birth. It's crazy to think about, overwhelming at least. He has written the story of our lives and we are living it out, expected to trust in Him and His path for us.

Sometimes it seems impossible to trust in the plan, especially when it disagrees with what we want. Sometimes (many times) it is so painful that we just want to wake up from the nightmare and live out the life we had planned. Sometimes the plan makes us angry and discouraged and honestly we just want to throw a tantrum like a toddler. And that's OK. Sometimes we question and we doubt and we scream and we cry out *why?* and we just can't comprehend the reason or how any ounce of good can come out the plan we are chosen to live. But still, He says *trust.*

Living those horrible days leads to being able to live the tolerable days, and then those tolerable days lead to days where joy shows up at least momentary, and day after day, month after month, year after year, the pain is less, the joy is more, and goodness begins to show its face in the most unexpected of ways and we believe again that life is GOOD. God is ALWAYS good. And His plan produces the harvest for Heaven and all its glory. Trusting that He knows all and believing our pain results in Kingdom growth, we focus on Heaven and remind ourselves this is all temporary.

And so, we find joy every day. In the little things, the big things, all the things. I appreciate the good and the bad and I learn to trust Him more through it all. I try to cherish everything more knowing this is all temporary and can change any second. I am many times fearful because of the happiness in my heart and in my new love and I remind myself to just breathe and trust that God's plan reigns and no matter what, Heaven is still there.

I live every day thankful for every breath I breathe, every life experience — good and bad, every ounce of joy He has allowed into my heart, every precious memory of Chris and our life and love and our family and friends, every step I took on the days I didn't think I could stand, and every road that led me to finding Darron and his kids and the plans for our life together that a couple of years ago was unimaginable. Today and always, I am thankful.

The gratitude for the blessings in my life flows out of my heart as I see how God has worked everything out for this moment in time. Not that He wanted any of us to experience the soul-crushing pain we've endured. But that He truly created this masterpiece of beauty out of the ashes and revealed to me that if only I trust and follow Him and His will for my life, the rewards will come.

Has any of it been easy? No. Has it been worth it? Absolutely! None of us (thank you Lord) knows what tomorrow will bring and the challenges and struggles that might await us there. What good would come out of knowing anyway? Being able to place that trust in Him and focus on the moment and find joy right now seems to be the best way, at least for me. That's where my comfort and peace reside and the place fear is not welcome or allowed.

The purpose of this addition to my book is to hopefully reiterate how God's plan (although sometimes painful) creates beauty in a multitude of ways, and how when we can fully trust in His plan and His will for our life and the lives of those around us, we will find some peace, even in the most painful of days. For me to be able to look back at the last five years of my life, to see how His plan has brought me and those I love to this moment in time, to see how He has held us and comforted us and carried us and led us to where we are now, I see a showering of His blessings and love. I see that He is always good, always in control, always speaking to each one of us if only we listen, and always leading us to the path we were born to walk. For me to see how significant the last five years have been in spiritual growth, personal growth, and how He has taken so many broken pieces and has created a new masterpiece out of the pain, it all overwhelms me with gratitude and joy. It makes me so anxious to see His story continue to be told, to be experienced by us, to stand one day before His majestic presence and our eyes be completely opened and to truly understand the glory and harvest that came from all these experiences we call life. For me, knowing that truth helps me push forward without as much fear. It helps me trust Him more, focus on Heaven more, cherish every second more, and love those I love more. I pray that my experiences and being able to share some lessons I have learned through my path, will carry into someone else's life in a way of comfort and hope and peace.

I pray for each of you who have taken the time to read a life-changing portion of my story, especially if you know the same pain, I pray that you continually draw nearer to the One who is the ultimate healer and comforter. I pray that your focus can truly be on eternal rewards and that you can trust that our pain is for a purpose, even though we sometimes cannot see it. I pray that you can learn to live in this moment and find the joy in now, without fear of the future. I pray that you pray for all the help He can give you that no one else can. I pray that you don't forget how much you need Him through the hard times and that you need Him just as much in the happy ones (I pray that continuously). May you see every day that God is good. That He doesn't want us to hurt. That He has all of us in His hands and He is in control. That His story is sometimes painful, but always with rewards. May you find all the blessings God is showering down upon you and may you soak them all up and be truly thankful for each and every one. And lastly, may you take all the experiences, good or bad, through the mountain highs and the valley lows, may you take them all in stride and learn all the lessons, knowing Heaven is near and this is all temporary, and just enjoy the sweet ride of life until that sweet, precious day. What a day it will be! God bless you all.

Andrea

ACKNOWLEDGMENTS

My heart is filled with so much gratitude, it would take a whole other book to get it all out. So many have inspired me and encouraged me in all of this, and I am forever thankful.

First and foremost, my Heavenly Father deserves it all. I cannot do anything without Him and His love. The good Lord has held me up on days my body was not capable. He has restored me a multitude of times and has never quit me and has always provided. I continually fail Him, but still…He loves my undeserving self anyway. He blesses me anyway. He is a proud Father anyway. The Lord God above gets every ounce of credit for me even functioning at all, and for that and so much more He deserves all the glory.

Thank you Lord for providing the words through the power of the Holy Spirit, and for the comfort when those words were typed through tear-stained eyes, and I wasn't sure I was capable or strong enough. You knew, You provided and You sustained. It's all you Lord.

Second, my family deserves every thank you my human self can provide. God truly showered down a huge blessing when He chose these souls for my life partners, and they too have held me up many days I didn't feel capable. Their support is unwavering, their love is unconditional, and their actions have shown me I couldn't ask for more in a family. God did so BIG when He picked them for me.

To mine and Chris' children, thank you. Thank you for understanding when I didn't feel like cooking or cleaning or even getting out of bed some days. Thank you for wanting to protect me and trying to keep worry from me and just wanting to see me smile. Thank you for the smiles, and the laughs and the fun and crazy times that helped drown the pain. Thank you for always letting me know you love me and that you appreciate me. I know you have gained appreciation for a parent that most kids never do. I am such a proud mother of how you have carried yourselves and indeed conquered life as far as I'm concerned. Averee, Brody and Lilly Williamson, you are my heroes and I am indebted to you forever.

To my parents, you have given me more than I could ever repay. I've never had to ask you to help me—you just have—without hesitation or condition. I owe everything to you, and yet you are so unselfish you don't expect any returns from me. Thank you isn't enough, but I hope you know the gratitude I feel for you overflows from the depths of my soul. When I say God gave me the best parents, I do not exaggerate at all. Always and forever, thank you Rufus and Sharon Johnson.

To Chris' family, who is also my family, thank you for always loving me and accepting me and supporting me, and for always having my back. Thank you for raising such an amazing Christian man, and for teaching him the right things that shaped him into the son, husband, father and friend he was. I hope I have made you proud in honoring and remembering Chris, and in raising our kids. What a blessing it is to be a forever part of your wonderful family.

To Darron Hood, my new love and my future. Goodness is always the right word for what I feel. You came into my life and the kids' lives in such an unexpected and wonderful way and we have forever been changed for the better because of you and your kids. Thank you for loving me and being patient with me and always seeing the best in me. Thank you for supporting me and understanding more than anyone else ever could. I'll spend the rest of my life trying to give back to you what you have me. Thank you from the depths of my soul, sweet man.

To friends and church family and acquaintances, thank you for every kind gesture. Prayers, messages, meals and every act of kindness. For every card and gift and reminder you were thinking of us and loving us, thank you. To those of you who messaged me to say, "I want to take you to lunch." To those who anonymously paid for meals when we've been out or handed me money or sent checks in the mail to just try and make life easier. To those who have donated for my kids to have decreased tuition for school. To those who have not had to say a word, but have just hugged us and shown your love. Thank you, thank you, thank you.

To the respected and honorable men and women at the Florence Electricity Department and at the IBEW Local Union 558, I am in awe of your hearts. From your presence at the emergency room that June fifth night, to helping cover my husband at the cemetery, to honoring his memory and checking on me and the kids, to giving your time and money and tears because you truly loved Chris, thank you. I will always respect you and love you and remember each of you with admiration. Thank you for making life easier, and for helping me and the kids heal in ways you're not even aware of. When I think of you, I smile. When I see each of you, I see Chris. I know you will always remember and will never forget. What a blessing.

To Jeanne Foust, who took this work from me after many months of exhausted reading of its' words, and spent hours editing the words and passing her insight to me, thank you friend. I couldn't think of anyone I would entrust more with this treasure of mine. Thank you for your knowledge and your heart, your wisdom and your love. I'll never forget that funny conversation between you and Chris and Lilly that June fourth night on the sidewalk at church. It's funny and beautiful how God works it all together. I know in my heart that conversation wasn't a coincidence at all. Thank you for the time you spent reading these words and praying over them and for just being the Christian woman you are. Thank you isn't enough.

To Katie Rickard, who took the incredibly beautiful photograph that is the front cover of this book, it is absolutely one of the most painful yet beautiful pictures I have ever looked at. To see Chris' boots and hard hat, the beautiful representation of his job, the loss of his presence and the magnificent sunset behind them all in one image, what an impact. Thank you for capturing it and for also taking the headshot on the back cover. I appreciate the ways you have helped me in all of this and in capturing images I forever hold dear to my heart.

To Leann Durden, who excitedly and wholeheartedly helped me with the cover design of this work, thank you for being not only a great encourager, but a trusted friend. Again, the Lord works. I do not find it a coincidence that we are connected in several ways. You came along in this work at the perfect time, when I needed a push to get to the finish line. What a blessing! You are a true light Leann and I'm thankful for you and your contribution to this book.

Lastly, thank you to each one of you for reading our story — God's story. Thank you for letting me speak to you through the words God placed on my heart and soul. Thank you for taking the time to somewhat walk through the journey with me and I pray it touched your heart in a positive way.

And once again, and over and over for the rest of my life — Thank you Lord.

Made in the USA
Columbia, SC
02 December 2019

84215538R00124